Golden Delicious Games
for the APPLE™ Computer

Golden Delicious Games
for the APPLE™ Computer

HOWARD FRANKLIN

JOANNE KOLTNOW

LEROY FINKEL

John Wiley & Sons, Inc.

New York • Chichester • Brisbane • Toronto • Singapore

Publisher: Judy V. Wilson
Editor: Dianne Littwin
Composition and Make-up: Cobb/Dunlop, Inc.

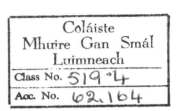
Any questions concerning the material in this book should be referred to the Publisher, John Wiley & Sons, and not to Apple Computer, which is not responsible for and was not involved in the preparation of this book. Apple is a trademark of Apple Computer, Inc., Cupertino, California.

Library of Congress Cataloging in Publication Data

Franklin, Howard.
    Golden delicious games for the Apple Computer.

    (Wiley self-teaching guides)
    Includes index.
    1. Apple II (Computer)—Programming. 2. Basic (Computer programming language) I. Finkel, LeRoy. II. Koltnow, Joanne. III. Title.
    QA76.8.A662F7   001.64'2   81-23074
    ISBN 0-471-09083-2   AACR2

Printed in the United States of America

82 83 10 9 8 7 6 5 4 3

Contents

Preface

Golden Delicious Games for the APPLE* Computer includes new games, enhancements to familiar games, and suggestions for programming projects to try. It is designed for those familiar with the BASIC language who want to write more interesting programs. You may be a parent, teacher, student, or simply a computer enthusiast.

We will provide you with well-designed routines to create sounds or color patterns, to filter data as it is entered, or to disable certain keys. These routines can be used as additions to your existing programs or as building blocks for new ones. We will also incorporate the routines into stand-alone programs that are actual games you can play. Both the routines and the stand-alone programs will be models of good programming style. They will also promote, by example, our belief in the importance of user-friendly computer programs.

Type the routines as they appear in the text. Save them, using the names we have given. This will allow us to take advantage of earlier work when we are building bigger routines, and it will save you retyping time. To get the most from the book, read the chapters sequentially.

Using this Book with Your Computer

To use this book, you will need an APPLE II computer with the APPLESOFT (FP) BASIC language. Some of our programs are fairly small, requiring no more than 16K memory. However, most will require 32K. The book is designed for use with a disk drive, on which to store the programs and routines discussed. Those of you with a cassette system will find that saving programs is a lot more complex. If you are using a disk system, it does not matter which Disk Operating System (DOS) you use—3.2 or 3.3.

---

*APPLE and APPLESOFT are trademarks of Apple Computer, Inc.

A Note About Computer Games

Few computer games in use these days are really new. Their origins can be traced to games written for large computers (the only computers available ten to fifteen years ago). These early games were played using teletype terminals and, thus, were text-line oriented. When you notice text scrolling off the screen during a game, remember that a roll of teletype paper had no screen size limitation. Programmers knew that if players missed an instruction they could look back and find it.

We bring this up for two reasons. First, it is useful to know how something got to be the way it is. Computer games have a history, and, when we can, we will point out the origins of games we discuss.

Second, because so many current games are simply microcomputer adaptations of the earlier, teletype-based games, they have some drawbacks—like text scrolling off the screen. Also, they do not take full advantage of the micros' capabilities. Throughout the book, we will suggest ways you can improve existing games by using your APPLE's features.

CHAPTER ONE

Musical Notes
and Sound Effects

This chapter introduces some of the basic sound capabilities of your APPLE computer and provides sound-effect routines you can add to existing programs. These routines are then used as the basis for new programs with suggested variations you can make.

Program runs are not included in this book. It is impossible to include a run of a program that produces sounds; it is difficult to include a run of a program that moves colored images. It is, however, appropriate to discuss the choices we have made for the way the program responds to the player. Thus, the chapters include discussions of particular player–program dialogues.

The APPLE produces sound by very quickly clicking a switch on and off inside the computer. It produces a tone by projecting a long series of these tiny clicks through the speaker. Changing the number of clicks per second changes the tone. All the different sounds your APPLE makes come from these clicks projected through the speaker. For example, a sound roughly equivalent to an A on a musical scale requires 440 clicks per second.

BELL

Your APPLE will produce a beep tone, sometimes called a bell, if you type Control-G. (Hold down the CTRL key while you type G.) Do this a few times and listen to the sound. Control-G makes this sound by using a program stored in the computer that produces a particular series of clicks.

Did you notice that the G key is also labeled BELL? The label is an artifact from the days when teletype terminals had bells inside, and typing Control-G actually rang the bell. These days, the "bell" usually doesn't sound like a bell, but most terminals have some kind of audible tone produced by typing Control-G.

Suppose you want to use the beep sound to celebrate a winning move in a game. You can include Control-G in a PRINT statement, as part of your program. However, control characters don't appear in a program listing, so while the characters would be there in your PRINT statements, they would be missing from the listing.

```
PRINT "YOU GOT IT!!"
(invisible Control G)
```

While this isn't bad, it could be annoying or confusing when you look at your listing. Fortunately, there is an alternative. CHR$(7) is the ASCII equivalent for Control-G, and these characters will appear in a listing. Use CHR$(7) within a PRINT statement like this:

```
PRINT "YOU GOT IT!!"; CHR$(7)
PRINT CHR$(7);"YOU";CHR$(7)'"GOT";
CHR$(7);"IT!!!";CHR$(7)
```

You can see, however, that typing CHR$(7) can become tiresome very quickly, and besides, you might forget which number to use. If you define a string variable for the beep, the PRINT statements are easier to type. We'll use BL$ as the variable for the beep:

```
10 BL$ = CHR$(7)
20 PRINT BL$; "YOU ";BL$;"GOT ";BL$;"IT!!!";BL$
```

PAUSE

If you try this on your APPLE, you'll notice that the words and the tones occur almost simultaneously. The PRINT statement is executed so rapidly that it's hard to tell that the tones follow the words. In fact, if you want to play a tone several times, you'll find that the sounds blend together. (PRINT BL$;BL$;BL$ sounds like one beep instead of three.)

The SPEED command controls the rate at which characters are displayed on the screen in a PRINT statement. SPEED = 255 is the fastest; SPEED = 0 is the slowest. When no speed is specified, the default speed (255) is used. Here is an interesting way to use the SPEED command to control the delay between bells:

```
10   REM  ...BEEP PAUSE...
11 :
12   REM  INSERT A PAUSE BETWEEN BEEPS USING 'SPEED'
13 :
100  BL$ = CHR$ (7)
110  SPEED= 0
120  PRINT BL$;BL$;BL$
130  SPEED= 255
```

RUN it with the speed set at 0. Then RUN the program again, changing the speed in line 110 to 50, 100, 150, etc.

BELL GAMES

Simple programs that use the beep are easy to design. For instance, teachers or parents of young children might use the beep in a program to teach counting. One such program asks the player to pick a number from 1 to 10. Then the program displays the counting series to reach that number, beeping to punctuate each number. If, for instance, the child pressed 5, the program would beep and display 1, beep and display 2, beep and display 3, etc. The child playing counts the beeps while watching the number series appear on the screen. Here is the program.

```
10   REM   ...INPUT BEEPS...
11  .
12   REM   BEEP # OF TIMES INPUT
13  :
100  L = 1: REM   MINIMUM # OF BEEPS
110  H = 5: REM   MAXIMUM
200  TEXT : HOME
210  PRINT "PLEASE PICK A NUMBER FROM ";L;"
     TO ";H;: INPUT ": ",N
220  IF N < L OR N > H THEN 200
230  PRINT
300  PRINT "COUNT THE BEEPS...": PRINT : PRINT
310  FOR J = 1 TO 1000: NEXT : REM  PAUSE BEFORE FIRST BEEP
320  FOR J = 1 TO N
330  SPEED= 0
340  PRINT "   ";: REM  WASTE TIME WITH 2 BLANKS
350  SPEED= 255
360  PRINT J;
370  PRINT CHR$ (7);
390  NEXT
500  PRINT : VTAB 18
510  PRINT "PRESS RETURN TO TRY AGAIN... ";
520  GET Z$
530  IF Z$ = CHR$ (27) THEN END : REM  CHECK FOR ESC
540  GOTO 200
```

SAVE this program, as INPUT BEEPS, then RUN it.

Look at the program listing. How would you change the maximum number of beeps to 20?

—————————————

110 H = 20

This is a slightly unusual program because the player is always in control. In most educational programs and many games, the computer is in control. In fact, the computer is usually testing rather than teaching. As you write programs, think about who should be in control during the game. It's usually more fun for the players if they are in control.

A more conventional variation on the beep and number idea is one in which the program selects a number, beeps that many times, then asks the player to type the number of beeps. Notice that this new program tests the player's ability to count beeps. It also gives encouragement if the guess is close to the right answer (see lines 120 and 430 below).

Instead of entering the entire program, we can modify the last program, INPUT BEEPS, as follows:

Delete lines 220, 230, and 360.

Insert these lines. (Some will be changes to make to other lines.)

```
10   REM   ...COUNT BEEPS-INPUT BEEPS...
11
100 L = 4. REM  MINIMUM # OF BEEPS
110 H = 16: REM  MAXIMUM
120 C = 1: REM  HOW CLOSE FOR "ENCOURAGEMENT"
210 N =  INT ((H - L + 1) *  RND (1)) + L: REM  # OF BEEPS
380  HTAB 1
400  INPUT "NOW, HOW MANY BEEPS WAS THAT? ";G
410  PRINT
420  IF G = N THEN  PRINT "YOU GOT IT!!!": GOTO 500
430  IF  ABS (G - N) < = C THEN  PRINT
     "CLOSE, BUT NOT QUITE... THERE WERE ";N;".": GOTO 500
440  PRINT "PLAY AGAIN... THERE WERE ";N;"."
```

SAVE this program as COUNT BEEPS and RUN it.
How would you change the "encouragement" variable to 3?

— — — — — — — — —

```
120 C = 3
```

OTHER SOUNDS

While the beep offers interesting programming possibilities for you
to experiment with, your APPLE can make many other sounds as
well. As noted earlier, the number of clicks per second (frequency)
determines the pitch of the tone. Thus, changes in the click frequency change the tone produced by the computer.

   First, enter the following and SAVE it as NEXTDATA MODULE. It
allows READ DATA to begin at any line number. You can also use
this module in your other programs to RESTORE the DATA pointer
to a specific line number. (See Appendix B for additional explanation.)

```
10   REM   ...NEXTDATA MODULE...
11 :
12   REM   NEXT READ FROM ANY LINE #
13 :
18991 :
18992 :
18993   REM   ** NEXT DATA FROM LINE Z **
18994   REM   ENTRY: Z  LINE #
18999 :
19000   IF YR% THEN 19200:
        REM   CHECK IF NEXT DATA ROUTINE ALREADY LOADED
19010 YR% = 770: REM   NEXT DATA ADDRESS
19097 :
19098   REM   NEXT DATA ROUTINE WRITTEN IN MACHINE CODE
19099 :
19100   POKE 770,173: POKE 771,0: POKE 772,3: POKE 773,133:
        POKE 774,80: POKE 775,173: POKE 776,1: POKE 777,3
19110   POKE 778,133: POKE 779,81: POKE 780,32: POKE 781,26:
        POKE 782,214: POKE 783,165: POKE 784,155: POKE 785,24
19120   POKE 786,105: POKE 787,4: POKE 788,133: POKE 789,125:
        POKE 790,165: POKE 791 156: POKE 792,105: POKE 793,0
19130   POKE 794,133: POKE 795,126: POKE 796,96
19200 Z% = Z / 256: POKE YR% - 2,Z - 256 * Z%:
        POKE YR% - 1,Z%: REM   LINE #
19210   CALL YR%
19220   RETURN
60000 :
60010   REM *COPYRIGHT 1981 BY HOWARD FRANKLIN, PALO ALTO, CA *
60020 :
```

SAVE this program as NEXTDATA MODULE.

This is the first of several "black box" routines we will give you. The term "black box" is used to describe something whose performance is understandable, but whose operation is not. Our "black box" routines are written in machine code. As we introduce them, we will tell you what they do, but not how they work, because they are too complicated to explain here. For those who are interested, refer to Appendix B. Most of you, however, will just use them unexplained, to make your programming easier.

Add the following to NEXTDATA MODULE:

```
10   REM   ...SOUND MODULE-NEXTDATA MODULE...
11 :
12   REM   SOUND MODULE TO PLAY ALPHABETIC STRINGS AND GENERATE
        SOUND EFFECTS
13 :
12991 :
12992 :
12993   REM   ** SOUND A PITCH FOR A SET DURATION **
12994   REM   ENTRY: WP  PITCH #
12995   REM              (WP=0 AND ROUTINE NOT LOADED =
                              INITIALIZATION ONLY)
12996   REM          WD  DURATION
12999 :
13000   IF WR% THEN 13200: REM   CHECK IF SOUND ROUTINE
        ALREADY LOADED
13010 WR% = 800:WP% = 799:WD% = 797: REM   SOUND, PITCH,
        DURATION ADDRESSES
13020 Z = 13100: GOSUB 19000: REM   SET READ DATA POINTER
13050 Z = WR%: REM   LOAD SOUND ROUTINE
13060   READ Z1: IF Z1 ) = 0 THEN POKE Z,Z1:Z =
        Z + 1: GOTO 13060
13070   IF WP = 0 THEN RETURN : REM   TRAP FOR
        INITIALIZATION ONLY
```

```
13097 :
13098   REM   SOUND ROUTINE WRITTEN IN MACHINE CODE
13099 :
13100   DATA   172,31,3,185,73,3,141,31,3,160,0,238,29,3,238,
        30,3,174,31,3,173,48,192

13110   DATA   136,208,10,206,29,3,208,5,206,30,3,240,5,202,240,
        234,208,238,96
13117 :
13118   REM   PITCHES
13119 :
13120   DATA   255,242,228,215,203,192,181,171
13130   DATA   161,152,143,135,127,120,113,107
13140   DATA   101,95,90,85,80,75,71,67
13150   DATA   63,59
13190   DATA   -1: REM   FLAG TO STOP READING DATA
13200   Z% = WD / 256: POKE WD%,WD - 256 * Z%: POKE WD%
        + 1,Z%: REM   DURATION
13210   POKE WP%,WP: REM   PITCH #
13220   CALL WR%
13230   RETURN
13292 :
13293   REM   * PLAY STRING OF ALPHABETIC LETTERS *
13294   REM   ENTRY: Z$   STRING
13295   REM          WD   DURATION
13299 :
13300   IF LEN (Z$) = 0 THEN   RETURN : REM   EMPTY STRING
13310   FOR W = 1 TO  LEN (Z$)
13320   WP = ASC ( MID$ (Z$,W,1)) - 64: REM   NEXT LETTER
13330   IF WP > = 1 AND WP < = 26 THEN   GOSUB 13000:
        REM   PLAY IF IN RANGE
13340   NEXT
13350   RETURN
13382 :
13383   REM   * SOUND EFFECTS *
13384   REM   ENTRY: W1   LENGTH OF EACH TONE ()=0)
13385   REM          W2   STEP BETWEEN TONES ()>0)
13386   REM               (W2=0 AND ROUTINE NOT LOADED =
        INITIALIZATION ONLY)
13387   REM          W3   STARTING TONE (0/255)
13388   REM          W4   # OF TONES IN CYCLE
13389   REM          W5   1=CYCLE DOWN; -1=UP; 0=DOWN AND UP
13390   REM          W6   PAUSE BETWEEN REPETITIONS OF CYCLE
13391   REM          W7   # OF REPETITIONS OF CYCLE
13399 :
13400   IF WE% THEN 13500: REM CHECK IF EFFECTS ALREADY LOADED
13410   IF WR% = 0 THEN WP = 0: GOSUB 13000: REM   LOAD SOUND
        ROUTINE IF NECESSARY
13420   WE% = 809: REM   EFFECTS ADDRESS
13430   IF W2 = 0 THEN   RETURN : REM   TRAP FOR
        INITIALIZATION ONLY
13500   WH% = W1 / 256:WL% = W1 - 256 * WH%: REM   DURATION
        AS TWO BYTES
13510   IF W2 < = 0 THEN W2 = 1: REM   FORCE VALID W2
13520   IF W3 < 0 THEN W3 = 0: REM   FORCE VALID W3
13530   FOR Z = 1 TO W7: REM   # OF REPETITIONS
13540   Z% = W3 + W2 * W4: IF W5 < 0 THEN 13600:
        REM   TRAP FOR UP ONLY
13550   FOR Z1 = W3 TO Z% STEP W2: REM   CYCLE DOWN
13560   IF Z1 < = 255 THEN   POKE WP%,Z1: POKE WD%,WL%:
        POKE WD% + 1,WH%: CALL WE%: REM NEXT TONE IS IN RANGE
13570   NEXT
13600   IF W5 > 0 THEN 13650: REM   TRAP FOR DOWN ONLY
13610   FOR Z1 = Z% TO W3 STEP  - W2: REM   CYCLE UP
13620   IF Z1 < = 255 THEN   POKE WP%,Z1: POKE WD%,WL%: POKE
        WD% + 1,WH%: CALL WE%: REM
        NEXT TONE IS IN RANGE
13630   NEXT
13650   FOR Z1 = 1 TO W6: NEXT : REM   PAUSE BETWEEN CYCLES
13660   NEXT
13670   RETURN
60000 :
60010   REM   * COPYRIGHT 1981 BY HOWARD FRANKLIN,
        PALO ALTO, CA *
60020 :
```

Type it and SAVE it as SOUND MODULE. This is a collection of subroutines that can be used in other programs but that does not do anything by itself.

MUSICAL NOTES

Make the following changes to SOUND MODULE and you will have a program in which the number keys (1 though 8) correspond to notes on the musical scale:

Delete lines 13120 through 13150.

```
10   REM    ...KEYS1/8-SOUND MODULE...
11   .
12   REM   PROGRAM TO "PLAY" THE KEYS 1/8
13   .
100  GOSUB 13000  REM   INITIALIZE SOUND ROUTINE
200  TEXT : HOME
210  PRINT "'PLAY' A TUNE USING THE NUMBERS 1 TO 8"
220  PRINT
230  PRINT "PRESS RETURN TO END YOUR 'TUNE'..."
240  PRINT "PRESS ESC TO STOP PLAYING..."
250  PRINT
300  GET Z$
310  IF Z$ = CHR$ (13) THEN 500: REM   RETURN
320  IF Z$ = CHR$ (27) THEN  END : REM  ESC
330  IF Z$ < "1" OR Z$ > "8" THEN 300: REM  IGNORE OTHER KEYS
340  PRINT Z$;
350 WP =  ASC (Z$) - 48: REM   CONVERT TO 1/8
360 WD = 50: REM   DURATION
370  GOSUB 13000
380  GOTO 300
500  PRINT : VTAB 18
510  PRINT "PRESS RETURN TO TRY AGAIN... ";
520  GET Z$
530  IF Z$ = CHR$ (27) THEN  END : REM  ESC
540  GOTO 200
13120  DATA  255,228,203,192,171,152,135,127
```

SAVE this program as KEYS1/8. RUN it to play simple tunes using the keys 1 through 8. As you "play," the numbers you type appear on the screen. You can copy them to keep track of the tunes you like. As in our other programs, press RETURN to end your tune; press ESC to stop the program.

The SOUND MODULE routine instructs the computer to produce tones at a number of different frequencies. It works much the same as the internal routine activated when you type Control-G. This time, we chose frequencies that roughly correspond to the scale and used the numbers 1 through 8 to play the scale. The matching pattern is arbitrary and is assigned by the DATA statements in lines 13120 through 13150.

Play this series of notes, pausing when you come to an asterisk:
6545666 * 555 * 688 * 6545666655654. What is the tune?

— — — — — — — — — —

Mary had a little lamb.

By changing the DATA statements in lines 13120 through 13150,
we can create additional click frequencies. We can match them this
time to the letter keys, in alphabetical order. The routine that follows
provides a twenty-six-note chromatic scale.

Here are the statements that change the assignment of keys 1
through 8 to keys A through Z. Make the following changes to
KEYS1/8:

```
10   REM   ...KEYSA/Z-KEYS1/8...
11   :
12   REM   PROGRAM TO "PLAY" THE KEYS A/Z (ALPHABETICAL ORDER)
13   :
210  PRINT "'PLAY' A TUNE USING THE KEYS A THROUGH Z"
330  IF Z$ < "A" OR Z$ > "Z" THEN 300: REM  IGNORE OTHER KEYS
350  WP = ASC (Z$) - 64: REM  CONVERT TO A/Z
13120  DATA  255,242,228,215,203,192,181,171
13130  DATA  161,152,143,135,127,120,113,107
13140  DATA  101,95,90,85,80,75,71,67
13150  DATA  63,59
```

SAVE this program as KEYSA/Z. RUN it and play on the keyboard
using the keys A through Z. Listen to the sounds. When you find a
series of notes you like, copy the letters from the screen so you can
play your "song" again.

MUSICAL MESSAGE

Obviously, the next thing to have is a program that plays your
message from memory rather than from the keyboard. The following
program allows you to enter the series of tones you want from the
keyboard. The program plays the series when you press RETURN
instead of each time you press a key.

Make the following changes to KEYSA/Z: Delete lines 300 through 380, and add the following lines:

```
10   REM   ...MUSIC MESSAGE-KEYSA/Z...
11   :
12   REM  PROGRAM TO INPUT, THEN "PLAY"
 A STRING (A/Z ALPHABETICAL)
13   :
230   PRINT "ENTER 'TUNE' THEN PRESS RETURN TO PLAY."
240   PRINT
250   INPUT "TUNE: ",Z$
300   WD = 50: REM  DURATION
310   GOSUB 13300: REM  PLAY STRING
```

SAVE this program as MUSIC MESSAGE. RUN it, using some of the "tunes" you copied from before.

How about typing your name and listening to the computer "play" it? How do your city and state "sound?" A variation might ask for your name and then play it several times, perhaps alternating direction.

How would you alter the program so that the message was played three times, instead of just once?

— — — — — — — — — —

```
305 FOR J = 1 to 3
315 NEXT
```

Change MUSIC MESSAGE by adding the following lines:

```
10   REM   ...BACK AND FORTH-MUSIC MESSAGE...
11   :
12   REM  INPUT THEN "PLAY" A STRING BACK AND FORTH
13   :
110  BF = 1: REM  # OF TIMES BACK AND FORTH
250   INPUT "TUNE: ",F$
260   B$ = ""
270   IF  LEN (F$) THEN  FOR J = 1 TO  LEN (F$):B$ = B$ +
     MID$ (F$, LEN (F$) + 1 - J 1): NEXT : REM  REVERSE STRING
290   FOR J = 1 TO BF
305  Z$ = F$: REM  FORWARD
320  Z$ = B$: GOSUB 13300: REM  BACK
330   NEXT
```

SAVE this program as BACK AND FORTH and RUN it. Type A through Z as your tune and listen to it.

You have a program that will play your series of letters first the way you typed them, then again in the opposite direction. After you have experimented with a few words and phrases, try typing some palindromes to see how they sound. (A palindrome is a series of letters that reads the same in either direction. Two well-known palindromes are "Madam I'm Adam" and "A man a plan a canal Panama.")

1.   All the tones are the same length. What line do you change to make the tones longer or shorter?

2.   How do you change the number of times the line is played back and forth?

— — — — — — — — — —

1.   Line 300
2.   Change the value of BF in line 110

PIANO

When you are ready for a different keyboard, create the following PIANO program. This time each keyboard letter is associated with one note, left-to-right and bottom-to-top order, instead of alphabetical order.

To create PIANO, make the following changes to the program KEYSA/Z (not BACK AND FORTH, although these changes would change the BACK AND FORTH keyboard as well):

```
10   REM   ...PIANO-KEYSA/Z
11  :
12   REM   "PIANO" USING A/Z
13  :
210   PRINT "'PIANO' USING THE KEYS A THROUGH Z"
13120   DATA   171,203,228,152,90,143,135,127
13130   DATA   67,120,113,107,181,192,63,59
13140   DATA   101,85,161,80,71,215,95,242
13150   DATA   75,255
```

Save this program as PIANO. Again, all we have done is change the pitch assignment in lines 13120 through 13150.

Using this program, you can play your keyboard somewhat like a piano. (Except that the tones all have the same length and you can play only one note at a time.) See if it is easier to pick out your favorite tunes when the notes are arranged this way.

ELECTRIC ORGAN

One limitation of the previous programs is that the tones are of set duration. We can vary the length of all the tones, but we have not yet been able to vary the length of individual tones independent of each other.

The following program takes duration time to the other extreme. A tone lasts until a new key is pressed—in effect, imitating an electric organ.

Modify PIANO as follows:

```
10   REM   ...ORGAN-PIANO...
11  :
12   REM   ELECTRIC ORGAN
13  .
100   GOSUB 13700: REM   INITIALIZE ORGAN ROUTINE
210   PRINT "'ORGAN' USING THE KEYS A THROUGH Z"
370   GOSUB 13700
13692 :
13693  REM   * ORGAN *
13694  REM   ENTRY: WP  PITCH #
13695  REM
         (WP=0 AND ROUTINE NOT LOADED = INITIALIZATION ONLY)
13699 :
13700  IF WS% THEN 13900:
         REM   CHECK IF ORGAN ROUTINE ALREADY LOADED
13710 WS% = 882: REM   ORGAN ADDRESS
13720  IF WR% = 0 THEN W = WP:WP = 0: GOSUB 13000:WP = W:
         REM  LOAD SOUND ROUTINE (SAVING PITCH)
13730 Z = 13800: GOSUB 19000: REM   SET READ DATA POINTER
13750 Z = WS%: REM  LOAD ORGAN ROUTINE
13760  READ Z1: IF Z1 ) = 0 THEN  POKE Z,Z1:Z = Z + 1: GOTO 13760
13770  IF WP = 0 THEN  RETURN : REM  TRAP FOR INITIALIZATION ONLY
13797 :
13798  REM  ORGAN ROUTINE WRITTEN IN MACHINE CODE
13799 :
13800  DATA   172,31,3,185,73,3,141,31,3,173,0,192,48,14,
         174,31,3,173,48,192
13810  DATA   136,208,0,202,240,239,208,248,96
13890  DATA   -1: REM  FLAG TO STOP READING DATA
13900  POKE WP%,WP: REM  PITCH #
13910  CALL WS%
13920  RETURN
```

SAVE this program as ORGAN. Play it to see how it differs from PIANO.

SOUND EFFECTS

Finally, we are providing a very powerful SOUND EFFECTS routine. Because it offers so many possibilities, we will suggest a systematic way for you to explore it.

We can develop a huge variety of sound effects by adding the following to SOUND MODULE:

```
10   REM   ...SOUND EFFECTS-SOUND MODULE...
11 :
12   REM   SOUND EFFECTS DEVELOPER
13 :
100   GOSUB 13400: REM   INITIALIZE SOUND EFFECTS ROUTINE
210 W1 = 0
220 W2 = 1
230 W3 = 0
240 W4 = 10
250 W5 = 1
260 W6 = 200
270 W7 = 4
300   TEXT : HOME
310   PRINT : PRINT "LENGTH OF EACH TONE: ";W1
320   PRINT : PRINT "STEP BETWEEN TONES: ";W2
330   PRINT : PRINT "STARTING TONE: ";W3
340   PRINT : PRINT "# OF TONES IN CYCLE: ";W4
350   PRINT : PRINT "1=CYCLE DOWN; -1=UP; 0=UP AND DOWN: ";W5
360   PRINT : PRINT "PAUSE BETWEEN REPETITIONS: ";W6
370   PRINT : PRINT "# OF REPETITIONS: ";W7
500   PRINT : VTAB 18
510   PRINT "PRESS RETURN TO LISTEN... ";
520   GET Z$
530   IF Z$ = CHR$ (27) THEN END : REM   ESC
540   GOSUB 13400
600   PRINT : PRINT
610   PRINT "PRESS RETURN TO TRY NEW VALUES... ";
620   GET Z$
630   IF Z$ = CHR$ (27) THEN END : REM   ESC
700   TEXT : HOME
710   PRINT "FOR EACH PARAMETER, ENTER A NEW VALUE"
720   PRINT "OR PRESS RETURN TO KEEP THE OLD ONE."
810   PRINT : PRINT "OLD LENGTH OF EACH TONE: ";W1;"   NEW: ";:
      INPUT Z$: IF LEN (Z$) THEN W1 = VAL (Z$)
820   PRINT : PRINT "OLD STEP BETWEEN TONES: ";W2;"   NEW: ";:
      INPUT Z$: IF LEN (Z$) THEN W2 = VAL (Z$)
830   PRINT : PRINT "OLD STARTING TONE: ";W3;"   NEW: ";:
      INPUT Z$: IF LEN (Z$) THEN W3 = VAL (Z$)
840   PRINT : PRINT "OLD # OF TONES IN CYCLE: ";W4;"   NEW: ";:
      INPUT Z$: IF LEN (Z$) THEN W4 = VAL (Z$)
850   PRINT : PRINT "OLD DOWN/UP PARAMETER: ";W5;"   NEW: ";:
      INPUT Z$: IF LEN (Z$) THEN W5 = VAL (Z$)
860   PRINT : PRINT "OLD PAUSE BETWEEN: ";W6;"   NEW: ";:
      INPUT Z$: IF LEN (Z$) THEN W6 = VAL (Z$)
870   PRINT : PRINT "OLD # OF REPETITIONS: ";W7;"   NEW: ";:
      INPUT Z$: IF LEN (Z$) THENW7 = VAL (Z$)
890   GOTO 300
```

SAVE this program as SOUND EFFECTS. RUN the routine once or twice, and then come back to this discussion.

The routine displays the values that have been set for each parameter and then produces the sound effect when you press RETURN. Next, it asks for your changes to the parameters, one at a time. (Pressing RETURN retains the current value.)

The variety of sound effects you can get from this routine is immense. Although it's tempting to vary each parameter every time you run the routine, your exploration will be most productive if you vary only one or two parameters at a time. When you find sounds you like, play with the numbers to see if you can refine them further. Then make note of the numbers so you can use this routine, with these particular numbers assigned to the variables, in future programs.

First, see how the sound changes when you change the starting note. The possible tones in this cycle range from 0 (high) through 255 (low). We started with 0, the highest tone. Try some starting tones that are lower.

We originally set the number of notes in the cycle to 100; try shortening it. Did you notice that, as the cycle gets shorter, you begin to get bursts of sound? The step size is the number of tones between each tone. If you increase the step size, the resulting sound is less smooth.

Now, you might want to change the number of times the cycle repeats and the length of the pause between cycles. Neither of these changes will have a dramatic effect on the sound. However, changing the up/down parameter will significantly change what you hear. Your choices are 1 (down only), −1 (up only), and 0 (up and down).

At this point, you are probably becoming familiar with the parts of the routine you have explored. After you work with the routine for a while, you will be able to predict the kind of sounds different variable values will make.

By now, you should have a collection of number combinations written down that produce sounds you like. When you use this routine in a program, assign those numbers to the variables in the routine to produce the sound effects you want.

CHAPTER SUMMARY

In this chapter you saw how to use the bell and the SPEED statement. You were also given a stand-alone program that simulates a piano and another that simulates an organ.

The most useful program in this chapter is SOUND MODULE. This module allows you to produce musical sounds of all types and to make exotic sound effects. You will use SOUND MODULE in some of the programs presented later in this book.

Sound Subroutine Reference Summary

This chapter has shown you how to manipulate the various sound capabilities of your APPLE computer. Now we will show you how to incorporate sound into your own programs.

The variable names beginning with W, X, Y, and Z are used by our subroutine modules and should not be used in your programs except for communicating with our routines. Nor should your programs use line numbers between 10000 and 50000, because that is the area where our subroutine modules will be located.

Music Sounds Summary

To make music using the keyboard letters A to Z:
    Entry point = 13300
    Entry variables:
        Z$ string of letters
        WD tone duration
    Your entry to make music might look like this:

```
1220 Z$ = "GOLDEN DELICIOUS GAMES"
1230 WD = 100
1240 GOSUB 13300
1250 :
1260 : REM:PROGRAM CONTINUES
```

It is as easy as that!

Sound Effects Summary

To make sound effects, you can set as many as seven variables or use their default values.

Entry point = 13400
Entry variables:
    W1 length of each: $>= 0$
    W2 step between tones: > 0
    W3 starting tone: 0 through 255
    W4 number of tones in cycle
    W5 1 =cycle down; -1 =cycle up; 0=down and up
    W6 pause between repetitions
    W7 number of repetitions

Your program segment to make a sound effect might look like this:

```
1300 W1 = 4:W2 = 1:W3 = 50:W4 = 20
1310 W5 = 0:W6 = 200:W7 = 4
1320 GOSUB 13400
1330 :
1340 :REM: PROGRAM CONTINUES
```

CHAPTER TWO

Low-Resolution Graphics

In this chapter, you will learn the fundamentals of LO-RES and a number of different color effects. We will show you how to print dots of color on the screen. Then we will extend these ideas to colored lines, boxes, borders, and routines to cover the whole screen with color.

This chapter should help you become familiar enough with using LO-RES to add LO-RES capabilities to your own programs. While you may not be using the specific routines we develop here, you will be able to apply the ideas and create the effects you want in your own programs. (In Chapter 3, you will see how to create and manipulate "images" or patterns of LO-RES dots, allowing you to include additional effects in your programs.)

Your APPLE computer has sixteen colors that will display on your color TV or monitor. You control these colors using low-resolution graphics. Low resolution means that you can set only a limited degree of detail in your images. The smallest point you can address (do something with) is half the size of a text character printed on the screen. This is in contrast to high-resolution graphics that allow you to address much smaller points, thus getting greater detail in your images. However, only six colors are available in the HI-RES mode. We will discuss high-resolution graphics in Chapter 4.

You can use two modes in LO-RES. One mode allows forty lines of graphics and a four-line text window at the bottom of the screen. The other allows the whole screen (forty-eight lines) to be filled with graphics. We will use the first mode most often because it permits us to put instructions in text mode on the same screen as the picture.

Only by using the four-line text window can you mix color graphics and text on the screen. Later we will show you how to create block letters to write words or numbers using LO-RES.

COLOR GRAPHICS ON THE APPLE

You need only five commands to create LO-RES color effects: GR, COLOR, PLOT, HLIN, and VLIN.

GR tells the APPLE to go into the mixed-graphics mode. The screen is cleared and shows all black. (We will show you full-screen LO-RES graphics later in this chapter.)

COLOR sets a particular color. A color is set until you change it with another COLOR command. Type COLOR=4 and you will get APPLE color DARK GREEN. Use the following APPLE Color Table as a reference:

0	BLACK
1	MAGENTA
2	DARK BLUE
3	PURPLE
4	DARK GREEN
5	GRAY 1
6	MEDIUM BLUE
7	LIGHT BLUE
8	BROWN
9	ORANGE
10	GRAY 2
11	PINK
12	LIGHT GREEN
13	YELLOW
14	AQUAMARINE
15	WHITE

PLOT tells the APPLE to draw a colored dot at a particular point. When you are working in mixed-graphics mode, your screen is "divided" into a forty by forty point grid. The points are numbered from 0 to 39, with point 0, 0 at the upper left corner of the screen. In the number pair that specifies a point, the H (horizontal) coordinate is written first; the V (vertical) coordinate is written second. Thus, PLOT 3,9 tells APPLE to PLOT a dot in the third column across and in the ninth row down.

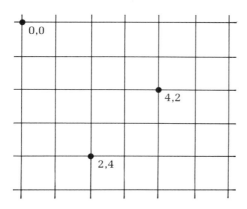

HLIN draws a horizontal line between two points at a specified vertical row. VLIN draws a vertical line between two points at a specified horizontal column. For example, HLIN 3,23 at 9 tells APPLE to draw a horizontal line from the third column to the twenty-third column, at the ninth row down.

To summarize: To draw a colored dot, go into graphics mode, set a color, and plot a point. To draw more than one dot of the same color, simply plot the next point. HLIN and VLIN plot horizontal and vertical lines, respectively. If you want to change the color, do so before you plot another point.

Try this program:

```
100  GR:COLOR= 4
110  HLIN 3,23 AT 9
120  VLIN 3,25 AT 23
130  END
```

COLORED DOTS

Below is a simple program for printing colored dots at random locations on the screen.

```
10   REM   ...COLOR DOTS...
11 :
100   GR : HOME
200   PRINT
210   PRINT "PRESS ANY KEY TO STOP ...";
300 H = INT (40 * RND (1))
400 V = INT (40 * RND (1))
500   COLOR= INT (16 * RND (1))
600   PLOT H,V
700 P = 200
710   FOR Z = 1 TO P: NEXT : REM  PAUSE
800   IF PEEK ( - 16384) ( 128 THEN 300: REM  NO KEYSTROKE
810   GET Z$: REM  THROW AWAY KEYSTROKE
```

Notice how the plotting locations are specified in line 300 (horizontal) and line 400 (vertical). Each coordinate is generated randomly from the numbers 0 to 39. The colors are generated randomly from 0 to 15 (line 500), so that all possible colors are included. The dot is actually plotted at line 600.

The formulas in lines 300 and 400 can be generalized so that you can generate a random number between any two numbers A and B. For future applications, use this generalized formula to generate random numbers.

LET R $=$ INT $((B-A+1)*RND(1))+A$

The last important item in this program is the pause in line 700. Changing the value in this variable changes the length of time before the next dot is displayed.

Type the preceding program and SAVE it as COLOR DOTS. RUN this COLOR DOT program. You can stop it by pressing any key. Mixed LO-RES mode will still be set, with only four lines of text at the bottom of the screen.

To return to full-screen text mode, type the command TEXT. Your screen will be filled with a variety of black and white images, some flashing. To rid your screen of this unattractive mess, type HOME. In future programming efforts, use the statement TEXT: HOME to enter text mode and clear the screen. To clear the screen and remain in LO-RES mode, use GR:HOME.

See what happens when you vary some of the parameters in COLOR DOTS.

1.   How can you change COLOR DOTS to make pink "snow" cover the ground?

2.   How can you alter COLOR DOTS to have yellow "stars" slowly appear above a horizon that is halfway up the screen?

3.   How would you fill a ten by ten dot rectangle in the center of the screen with purple dots?

— — — — — — — — — —

1.   Modify COLOR DOTS: 500 COLOR = 11
2.   Modify COLOR DOTS:

```
10   REM   ...YELLOW STARS-COLOR DOTS...
11
400  V =   INT (20 *  RND (1))
500   COLOR= 13
700  P = 1000
```

3.   Set the color to purple. Set the H and V coordinates so that both vary from 15 to 24.

```
10   REM   ...PURPLE RECTANGLE-COLOR DOTS...
11
300  H =   INT (10 *  RND (1)) + 15
400  V =   INT (10 *  RND (1)) + 15
500   COLOR= 3
```

You might use a variation of the dot routine in your own programs. Would you ever need to represent the eyes of jungle animals appearing in the night forest? You could have dark green and yellow dots appearing on a black screen. How about looking down at coins dropping into a wishing well? You could make yellow dots appear within a circular area in the center of the screen. In both cases, you could use a FOR-NEXT loop to control the number of dots that appear. Here is the complete listing of WISHING WELL:

```
10   REM   ...WISHING WELL...
11  :
100   GR : HOME
120   RA = 16: REM  RADIUS OF WELL
130   R2 = RA * RA: REM  RADIUS SQUARED
140   H0 = 19: REM  H-POS OF CENTER
150   V0 = 19: REM  V-POS
200   PRINT
210   PRINT "PRESS ANY KEY TO STOP ...";
300   REM  FIRST SELECT H,V IN A SQUARE CENTERED AT
      (H0,V0) WITH SIDE = 2*RA
310   H =  INT (2 * RA *  RND (1)) + H0 - RA
400   V =  INT (2 * RA *  RND (1)) + V0 - RA
410   REM  SECOND CHECK IF (H,V) IS WITHIN THE CIRCLE
420   IF (H - H0) ^ 2 + (V - V0) ^ 2 > R2 THEN 310:
      REM  SELECT A NEW POINT IF IN SQUARE BUT NOT CIRCLE
500   COLOR= 13
600   PLOT H,V
700   P = 1
710   FOR Z = 1 TO P: NEXT : REM  PAUSE
800   IF  PEEK ( - 16384) < 128 THEN 300: REM  NO KEYSTROKE
810   GET Z$: REM  THROW AWAY KEYSTROKE
```

These are just a few of the possibilities you can program using this basic dot routine.

Another way you can alter this program is to use a random, rather than fixed, time delay for the value of P in line 700. Select a range for the delay, and then use the formula we gave you earlier (page 000).
1.   If you want to print only dots of medium blue and orange, how would you change the routine? (Refer to the color table on page 00.)

2. Suppose you still want medium blue and orange dots, but you want blue to be three times as likely to appear. How would you change the routine?

--- --- --- --- --- ---

```
1. 500 COLOR = 6
   510 IF RND(1)<.5 THEN COLOR = 9
```
(The .5 gives each color a 50–50 chance.)

```
2. 500 COLOR = 6
   510 IF RND(1)<.25 THEN COLOR = 9
```
(One chance in four is controlled by the .25.)

Here is a program that uses the dot routine to "grow" wildflowers in a bare field. We have chosen three flower colors (red, yellow, and purple) and assigned them at 20% each. Then, we assigned dark green at 40%.
Modify original COLOR DOTS:

```
10   REM   ...FLOWERS-COLOR DOTS...
11 :
400  V =   INT (30 *  RND (1)) + 10
500  Z =   INT (100 *  RND (1)) + 1:  REM  1/100
510  COLOR= (Z (  = 20) * 1 + (Z > 20 AND Z
       (  = 40) * 13 + (Z > 40 AND Z ( = 60) * 3 + (Z > 60) * 4
```

Type this program and SAVE it as FLOWERS. Then RUN this program and watch the flowers cover the field. To assure that they don't also cover the sky, we limited the V coordinate so that the dots do not appear above V=10 (see line 400 above).

COLORED LINES

The only difference between plotting points and drawing lines is that points need only two coordinates whereas lines must have both endpoints specified. Because we are drawing only horizontal or vertical lines, the endpoint specification is simple.

Use HLIN and specify the starting and ending columns and the vertical distance from the top of the screen (the row). HLIN 10,20 at 5 draws a horizontal line from the tenth to the twentieth column, five rows down. VLIN 10,20 at 5 draws a vertical line from the tenth row to the twentieth row, in the fifth column from the left.

The following program creates lines instead of dots, and it builds on what you learned earlier. The program selects the endpoints (determining whether the line will be horizontal or vertical and how long it will be), the color of the lines, and the time delay between drawing lines.

Modify the original COLOR DOTS:

```
10   REM   ...COLOR LINES-COLOR DOTS...
11  :
300 H1 =   INT (40 *   RND (1))
350 H2 =   INT (40 *   RND (1))
400 V1 =   INT (40 *   RND (1))
450 V2 =   INT (40 *   RND (1))
600 D =   INT (2 *   RND (1)): REM   D =0 (HLIN), =1 (VLIN)
650   IF D = 0 THEN   HLIN H1,H2 AT V1
660   IF D = 1 THEN   VLIN V1,V2 AT H1
```

SAVE it as COLOR LINES. Try this program exactly as it appears. Then vary some of the parameters. How about limiting the colors (line 500)?

How would you change the program to limit the possible lengths of the lines?

_ _ _ _ _ _ _ _ _ _

Modify COLOR LINES as follows:

```
10   REM   ...LINE LENGTHS-COLOR LINES...
11
120 HL = 20. REM  MAXIMUM HLIN LENGTH
130 VL = 10: REM  VLIN
360  IF· ABS (H2 - H1) > HL THEN 350: REM  PICK AGAIN - TOO LONG
460  IF  ABS (V2 - V1) > VL THEN 450: REM  PICK AGAIN - TOO LONG
```

SAVE this program as LINE LENGTHS.

Do you think you would ever need to fill the screen with short, vertical lines? (They might represent people appearing out of nowhere.) You can eliminate horizontal lines from the routine by making this change to line 600:

600 D = 1

Another way to make this program interesting (and the earlier one, too) is to make it interactive. Currently, the values for all variables are created by the program. You can alter the program so that it accepts values from the keyboard. Make the following changes to LINE LENGTHS:

```
10    REM   ...INPUT COLORS-LINE LENGTHS...
11    :
150   CL = 1: REM   INITIAL COLOR
210   PRINT "PRESS ESC TO STOP ...";
500   Z$ = "ASDFGHJKLZXCVBNM"
510   GOSUB 1000: REM   CHECK KEYSTROKE
520   IF Z THEN CL = Z - 1: REM   UPDATE COLOR IF KEYSTROKE MATCHED
530   COLOR= CL
800   Z$ = CHR$ (27): REM   CHECK FOR ESC
810   GOSUB 1000
820   IF Z = 0 THEN 300
900   END
991   :
992   REM   * CHECK IF KEYSTROKE IS IN SET *
993   REM   ENTRY:  Z$  STRING OF KEYS TO MATCH
994   REM   EXIT:   Z   0 (NO MATCH) AND KEYSTROKE (IF ANY) NOT CLEARED
995   REM           Z   J (J-TH CHARACTER IN Z$) AND KEYSTROKE CLEARED
999   :
1000  Z = 0: REM   SET NO-MATCH FLAG
1010  Z1 = PEEK ( - 16384) - 128: REM   READ KEYSTROKE
1020  IF Z1 < 0 THEN  RETURN : REM   NO KEY PRESSED
1030  IF  LEN (Z$) = 0 THEN  RETURN : REM   NO CHARACTERS TO MATCH
1040  FOR Z2 = 1 TO  LEN (Z$)
1050  IF Z1 =  ASC ( MID$ (Z$,Z2,1)) THEN Z = Z2:  GET Z1$:
      REM   MATCH FOUND - CLEAR KEYSTROKE
1060  NEXT
1070  RETURN
```

SAVE this program as INPUT COLORS. RUN the program and watch the lines appear. They are all red. Now, as the program runs, type alphabet keys in the two bottom rows. (A through L or Z through M.) As you type, the colors will change. We have assigned one of the APPLE colors to each of the keys (see line 500). The assignment was arbitrary; we could have used an assignment scheme other than the rainbow one we chose.

Now, using this idea of changing where the routine gets the values for the variable, we can make the following change and have the number keys (1 through 9) provide the length of the horizontal line, and the keys Q through O provide the length of the vertical line. The keys to the left will generate short lines; those to the right, long lines.

Modify INPUT COLORS:

```
10    REM   ...INPUT LENGTHS-INPUT COLORS...
11    :
310   Z$ = "123456789"
320   GOSUB 1000
330   IF Z THEN HL = 2 * Z: REM   UPDATE HLIN LENGTH IF KEYSTROKE
340   Z = 1 - 2 *  INT (2 *  RND (1)): REM   +1, -1
350   H2 = H1 + Z * HL: REM   + OR - HL
360   IF H2 < 0 OR H2 > 39 THEN H2 = H1 - Z * HL:
      REM   - OR + IF OUT OF RANGE
410   Z$ = "QWERTYUIO"
420   GOSUB 1000
430   IF Z THEN VL = 2 * Z: REM   UPDATE VLIN LENGTH IF KEYSTROKE
440   Z = 1 - 2 *  INT (2 *  RND (1)): REM   +1, -1
450   V2 = V1 + Z * VL: REM   + OR - VL
460   IF V2 < 0 OR V2 > 39 THEN V2 = V1 - Z * VL:
      REM   - OR + IF OUT OF RANGE
```

SAVE this program as INPUT LENGTHS. RUN this program. You will probably find it enjoyable to interact with the program and to have immediate control over what is displayed on the screen. Remember, when you are designing programs, that interacting with the program is fun for the players.

You may have noticed when you were plotting color dots in LO-RES that the dots are not perfectly square—they are wider horizontally than they are high vertically. This is due to the structure of the LO-RES hardware. Similarly, vertical lines are "fatter and shorter" than horizontal lines drawn with the same values for length.

By now you probably realize that you can vary parameters within the routine to make other interesting effects: You can limit the colors and you can assign the horizontal and vertical lengths to the keys in different ways.

Boxes are one step beyond lines. You draw a line and then indicate which way and how far to "grow" it. The last program in this section prints colored boxes. Modify INPUT LENGTHS as follows:

```
10   REM   ...INPUT BOXES-INPUT LENGTHS...
11
650   IF D = 0 THEN   FOR Z = V1 TO V2 STEP  SGN (V2 - V1). HLIN H1,
      H2 AT Z  NEXT
660   IF D = 1 THEN   FOR Z = H1 TO H2 STEP  SGN (H2 - H1): VLIN V1,
      V2 AT Z  NEXT
```

SAVE it as INPUT BOXES. RUN it. Use keys 1 through 9 to vary the width, keys Q through O to vary the height, and A through M to vary the colors. You will see a direct relationship between what you do with the keys and what happens on the screen.

COLORING THE SCREEN

This section presents several other ways to color the screen. First, we will provide a routine to display a simple colored border, useful for calling attention to what's on the screen. This routine displays a colored border one line wide around the screen. Notice that the color is set in line 500.

SAVE this program as BORDER1. RUN it.

You can change BORDER1 to make it display borders of different colors that follow one after another. Here's how we did it:

```
10    REM    ...BORDER...
11  :
100   GR : HOME
500   COLOR= 1
600   HLIN 0,39 AT 0
610   VLIN 1,39 AT 39
620   HLIN 38,0 AT 39
630   VLIN 38,1 AT 0
```

Make BORDER1 a general-purpose program by deleting lines 600 through 630.

```
10    REM    ...BORDER2-BORDER1...
11  :
600  Z = 0: REM   0 DOTS FROM THE EDGE
610   GOSUB 900
820   END
891  :
892   REM  * LOW-RES BORDER *
893   REM   ENTRY: Z  # OF DOTS IN FROM THE EDGE
894   REM          COLOR SET
899  :
900  Z1 = 39 - Z
910   HLIN Z,Z1 AT Z
920   VLIN Z + 1,Z1 AT Z1
930   HLIN Z1 - 1,Z AT Z1
940   VLIN Z1 - 1,Z + 1 AT Z
950   RETURN
```

SAVE this program as BORDER2.

1.   How would you modify BORDER2 to set the border three dots in from the screen sides?

2.   How would you modify BORDER2 to make a double border with a space between the parts?

1. 600 Z = 3
2. One answer is: 620 Z = 2.
                              630 GOSUB 900

It's extremely useful to be able to wash the screen (fill it quickly and smoothly with a color). The following routine fills the screen by printing horizontal lines.

```
10   REM   ...WASH...
11   :
100   GR  :  HOME
500   COLOR= 1
600   FOR Z = 0 TO 39
610   HLIN 0,39 AT Z
620   NEXT
```

SAVE this program as WASH and RUN it.
How would you change the program to print stripes of alternating colors?

———————————

Modify WASH as follows:

```
10   REM   ...STRIPE-WASH...
11   :
500  C1 = 3:  REM   FIRST COLOR
510  C2 = 7:  REM   SECOND
520  C = C1:  REM   CURRENT
605   COLOR= C:C = C1 + C2 - C:  REM   CHANGE TO OTHER COLOR
```

The WASH routine provides a background color over which you can make other lines, dots, and even images, as you will see in the next chapter. You can easily change the background color in the WASH program by changing line 500.

Another way to color the screen is to print stripes around the screen in a spiral effect:

```
10   REM    ...SPIRAL...
11   :
100  GR : HOME
120  HO = 19: REM  H-POS OF CENTER
130  VO = 19: REM  V-POS
140  N = 19: REM  # OF LAYERS IN SPIRAL
150  P = 1: REM  PAUSE BETWEEN SEGMENTS
200  FOR J = N TO 0 STEP  - 1
210  H1 = HO - J: REM  LEFT EDGE OF CURRENT LAYER
220  H2 = HO + J + 1: REM  RIGHT
230  V1 = VO - J: REM  TOP
240  V2 = VO + J + 1: REM  BOTTOM
300  GOSUB 900
310  HLIN H1,H2 AT V1
350  GOSUB 900
360  VLIN V1 + 1,V2 AT H2
400  GOSUB 900
410  HLIN H2 - 1,H1 AT V2
450  GOSUB 900
460  VLIN V2 - 1,V1 + 1 AT H1
490  NEXT
820  END
892  :
893  REM  * SELECT COLOR FOR NEXT SEGMENT, THEN DELAY *
899  :
900  COLOR= 1
910  FOR Z = 1 TO P: NEXT
990  RETURN
```

SAVE this program as SPIRAL.

You may want to slow the printing so you can see the spiral more clearly. Do this by changing the delay in line 150:

```
150 P = 200
```

How would you change SPIRAL so it prints different colors on each bar of the spiral?

— — — — — — — — — —

```
900 COLOR = INT(16*RND(1))
```

SAVE this change as SPIRAL1.

Here is a modification to SPIRAL1 to have the spiral continue to close, then open:

```
10   REM   ...SPIRAL2-SPIRAL1...
11   :
190   PRINT : PRINT "PRESS ESC TO STOP ...";
500   COLOR= 0: FOR J = 0 TO N
510 H1 = H0 - J
520 H2 = H0 + J + 1
530 V1 = V0 - J
540 V2 = V0 + J + 1
600   GOSUB 910
610   VLIN V1 + 1,V2 - 1 AT H1
650   GOSUB 910
660   HLIN H1,H2 - 1 AT V2
700   GOSUB 910
710   VLIN V2,V1 + 1 AT H2
750   GOSUB 910
760   HLIN H2,H1 AT V1
790   NEXT
800   IF   PEEK ( - 16384) ( 128 THEN 200
810   GET Z$: IF Z$ ( ) CHR$ (27) THEN 200 : REM   NOT ESC
```

SAVE this as SPIRAL2. RUN it to see how it looks.

Modify SPIRAL2 to move the center and reduce the size of the spiral:

```
10   REM      SPIRAL3-SPIRAL2.
11   :
120 H0 = 10
130 V0 = 12
140 N = 4
```

SAVE this as SPIRAL3.

Try two spirals. Have them close and open at the same time. Although the following solution is tedious, it does produce a fine effect:

```
10   REM   ...TWO SPIRALS-SPIRAL3...
11   :
122 HC = 29: REM   INTERLEAVE SPIRAL #2
132 VC = V0
212 HA = HC - J
222 HB = HC + J + 1
232 VA = VC - J
242 VB = VC + J + 1
312   HLIN HA,HB AT VA
362   VLIN VA + 1,VB AT HB
412   HLIN HB - 1,HA AT VB
462   VLIN VB - 1,VA + 1 AT HA
512 HA = HC - J
522 HB = HC + J + 1
532 VA = VC - J
542 VB = VC + J + 1
612   VLIN VA + 1,VB - 1 AT HA
662   HLIN HA,HB - 1 AT VB
712   VLIN VB,VA + 1 AT HB
762   HLIN HB,HA AT VA
```

SAVE this as TWO SPIRALS. With a little imagination, you can see this as two eyes. Would you ever need a three-eyed monster to enhance a program?

COMBINING COLOR AND SOUND

Now let's combine sound with one of the screen coloring routines. Here's a program that makes ascending and descending scale sounds as a spiral closes and opens.

Modify SPIRAL2 as follows:

```
10  REM   ...SPIRAL SOUND-SPIRAL2...
11  :
180 WD = 10
920 WP = N + 1 - J
930   GOSUB 13000
```

Merge with SOUND MODULE. SAVE this as SPIRAL SOUND and RUN it.

With an additional change, you can have a program that drives your friends wild. The sound is slightly offset from the spiral, so they don't start and finish at the same time.

```
10  REM   ...SPIRAL CRAZY-SPIRAL SOUND...
11  :
170 CP = 1:CZ = .25
920 WP =   INT (CP)
940 CP = CP + CZ
950  IF CP > N + 2.25 THEN CZ =   - .25: GOTO 940: REM  UP TO DOWN
960  IF CP < 1 THEN CZ = .25: GOTO 940: REM  DOWN TO UP
```

Experiment on your own with adding LO-RES effects corresponding to the note change in the ORGAN program. How about displaying a colored dot each time you press a note (A through Z)? How about special color effects each time you press one of the number keys? (This is a little like using the pedals in a real organ.) For example, pressing the 1 key could signal to wash the screen with red; the 2 key could signal an orange wash, etc. How about triggering a spiral if a random key is pressed?

On the other hand, a simpler program would have the 1 key change the screen to another color that was selected at random.

As you can see, you can combine color with sound in a variety of ways to make them both more interesting.

FULL-SCREEN LO-RES GRAPHICS

Each of our programs has used a four-line text window at the bottom of the screen. To eliminate the text window and gain eight additional graphic lines, use these two statements in your programs:

```
10   REM   ...FULL LOWRES
11 :
100  GR . POKE  - 16302,0. REM  SET FULL-SCREEN LOWRES
110  COLOR= 0. FOR Z = 40 TO 47. HLIN 0,39 AT Z. NEXT
     REM  CLEAR BOTTOM 8 LINES
```

CHAPTER SUMMARY

This chapter introduced the LO-RES graphics statements and showed some simple applications. The WASH, BORDER, AND SPIRAL programs will be particularly useful when you write your own programs.

CHAPTER THREE

Graphic Images in LO-RES

This chapter deals specifically with making images—pictures and symbols—using low-resolution graphics. You can create an image and then save it to use in future programs. We will present some images and show you how to use them. Then we will show you how to create, change, and store your own unique images. Finally, we will include programs that incorporate and manipulate images.

The building block of the image is the dot introduced in the previous chapter. Because low-resolution images are made of these rectangular dots, they have the quality of children's drawings or of pictures drawn in cross-stitch. Children especially find LO-RES images very appealing.

IMAGE MODULE

The following IMAGE MODULE allows you to display images on the screen. You specify the position, the color, and the image; the module does the work. For your ease in getting started, we have included an alphabet and the numerals 0 to 9. Later in the chapter, we will show you how to create, save, and display additional images.

As you can see from the listing below, spacing is crucial to the appearance of the letters. Be very careful when you type the image portion of this routine, or your characters will be misshapen.

```
10   REM   ...IMAGE MODULE-NEXTDATA MODULE...
11 :
12   REM   IMAGE SUBROUTINES + IMAGE LIBRARY
13 :
14981 :
14982 :
14983   REM   * DISPLAY IMAGE IN LOW-RES *
14984   REM   ENTRY: XH  H-POS OF UPPER-LEFT-HAND-CORNER
14985   REM          XV  V-POS
14986   REM          XA  HORIZONTAL WIDTH
14987   REM          XB  VERTICAL HEIGHT
14988   REM          READ DATA POINTER SET TO IMAGE
14989   REM          COLORS SELECTED IN XC()
14990   REM          GRAPHICS MODE SELECTED
14991   REM   EXIT:  Z%  0 IMAGE FITS
14992   REM              1 ERROR - DOES NOT FIT
14999 :
15000   IF XH + XA > 40 OR XV + XB > 48 THEN Z% = 1: RETURN :
        REM  ERROR - DOES NOT F IT
15010 Z1 = XV: REM  FIRST V-POS
15020   REM   INITIALIZATION UNNECESSARY -
        FIRST REFERENCE TO XC() CAUSES "DIM XC(10)"

15030   READ Z$: IF Z$ = "-1" THEN Z% = 0: RETURN : REM  CHECK IF DONE
15040   FOR Z = 1 TO LEN (Z$): REM  PLOT EACH 1/9 CHARACTER
15050 Z% = ASC ( MID$ (Z$,Z,1)) - 48
15060   IF Z% > = 1 AND Z% < = 9 THEN  COLOR= XC(Z%):
        PLOT XH + Z - 1,Z1: REM  PLOT DOT
15070   NEXT
15080 Z1 = Z1 + 1: REM  NEXT V-POS
15090   GOTO 15030
15092 :
15093   REM   * GET IMAGE *
15094   REM   ENTRY: Z   IMAGE #
15095   REM   EXIT:  XA  HORIZONTAL WIDTH
15096   REM          XB  VERTICAL HEIGHT
15097   REM          READ DATA POINTER SET TO IMAGE
15099 :
15100 Z = 20000 + 100 * Z: GOSUB 19000: REM  SET READ DATA POINTER
15110   READ XA,XB: REM  FIRST TWO DATA ARE WIDTH AND HEIGHT
15120   RETURN
15191 :
15192   REM   * DISPLAY ONE IMAGE *
15193   REM   ENTRY: Z   IMAGE #
15194   REM          XH  H-POS OF ULHC
15195   REM          XV  V-POS
15196   REM          COLORS SELECTED IN XC()
15197   REM   EXIT:  Z%  0 IMAGE FITS
15198   REM              1 ERROR - DOES NOT FIT
15199 :
15200   GOSUB 15100: REM  SET READ DATA POINTER
15210   GOTO 15000: REM  DISPLAY IMAGE
15292 :
15293   REM   * CENTER STRING OF IMAGES *
15294   REM   ENTRY: X$  STRING
15295   REM          XV  V-POS OF ULHC
15296   REM          COLORS SELECTED IN XC()
15297   REM   EXIT:  Z%  0 IMAGES FIT
15298   REM              1 ERROR - DO NOT FIT
15299 :
15300   IF  LEN (X$) = 0 THEN  RETURN : REM  EMPTY
15310   IF XS = 0 THEN XS = 1: REM  INITIALIZE SPACE BETWEEN IMAGES
15320 X1 = - XS: REM  INITIALIZE LOW-RES WIDTH
15330   FOR X = 1 TO LEN (X$)
15340 Z = ASC ( MID$ (X$,X,1)): GOSUB 15100:
        REM  IMAGE #S IDENTICAL TO ASCII #S
15350 X1 = X1 + XA + XS: REM  UPDATE LOW-RES WIDTH
15360   NEXT
15370   IF X1 > 40 + XS THEN Z% = 1: RETURN : REM ERROR - DOES NOT FIT
15380 XH = 19 - INT (X1 / 2): REM  DISPLAY AT LEFT MARGIN
15390 :
15391   REM   * DISPLAY STRING OF IMAGES *
15392   REM   ENTRY: X$  STRING
```

```
15393   REM           XH  H-POS OF ULHC
15394   REM           XV  V-POS
15395   REM           COLORS SELECTED IN XC()
15396   REM  EXIT:  XH  UPDATED
15397   REM          Z%  0 IMAGES FIT
15398   REM              1 ERROR - DO NOT FIT
15399   :
15400   IF  LEN (X$) = 0 THEN  RETURN : REM  EMPTY
15410   IF  XS = 0 THEN XS = 1: REM  INITIALIZE SPACE BETWEEN IMAGES
15420   FOR X = 1 TO  LEN (X$)
15430   Z =  ASC ( MID$ (X$,X,1)): GOSUB 15200: REM  DISPLAY ONE IMAGE
15440   XH = XH + XA + XS: REM  UPDATE H-POS
15450   NEXT
15460   RETURN
15492   :
15493   REM  * WASH 40X40 SCREEN IN ONE COLOR *
15494   REM  ENTRY: COLOR SET
15499   :
15500   Z = 39: REM  HEIGHT
15510   FOR Z1 = 0 TO Z: HLIN 0,39 AT Z1: NEXT
15520   RETURN
24800   DATA  5,7: REM  0
24810   DATA  " 111"
24820   DATA  "1   1"
24830   DATA  "1  11"
24840   DATA  "1 1 1"
24850   DATA  "11  1"
24860   DATA  "1   1"
24870   DATA  " 111"
24880   DATA  "-1"
24900   DATA  5,7: REM  1
24910   DATA  "  1"
24920   DATA  " 11"
24930   DATA  "  1"
24940   DATA  "  1"
24950   DATA  "  1"
24960   DATA  "  1"
24970   DATA  " 111"
24980   DATA  "-1"
25000   DATA  5,7: REM  2
25010   DATA  " 111"
25020   DATA  "1   1"
25030   DATA  "    1"
25040   DATA  "   11"
25050   DATA  " 1"
25060   DATA  "1"
25070   DATA  "11111"
25080   DATA  "-1"
25100   DATA  5,7: REM  3
25110   DATA  "11111"
25120   DATA  "    1"
25130   DATA  "    1"
25140   DATA  "   11"
25150   DATA  "    1"
25160   DATA  "1   1"
25170   DATA  " 111"
25180   DATA  "-1"
25200   DATA  5,7: REM  4
25210   DATA  "   1"
25220   DATA  "   11"
25230   DATA  "  1 1"
25240   DATA  "1   1"
25250   DATA  "11111"
25260   DATA  "    1"
25270   DATA  "    1"
25280   DATA  "-1"
25300   DATA  5,7: REM  5
25310   DATA  "11111"
25320   DATA  "1"
25330   DATA  "1111"
25340   DATA  "    1"
25350   DATA  "    1"
25360   DATA  "1   1"
```

```
25370 DATA  " 111"
25380 DATA  "-1"
25400 DATA  5,7: REM  6
25410 DATA  "  111"
25420 DATA  " 1"
25430 DATA  "1"
25440 DATA  "1111"
25450 DATA  "1    1"
25460 DATA  "1    1"
25470 DATA  " 111"
25480 DATA  "-1"
25500 DATA  5,7: REM  7
25510 DATA  "11111"
25520 DATA  "     1"
25530 DATA  "    1"
25540 DATA  "   1"
25550 DATA  "  1"
25560 DATA  "1"
25570 DATA  "1"
25580 DATA  "-1"
25600 DATA  5,7: REM  8
25610 DATA  " 111"
25620 DATA  "1    1"
25630 DATA  "1    1"
25640 DATA  " 111"
25650 DATA  "1    1"
25660 DATA  "1    1"
25670 DATA  " 111"
25680 DATA  "-1"
25700 DATA  5,7: REM  9
25710 DATA  " 111"
25720 DATA  "1    1"
25730 DATA  "1    1"
25740 DATA  " 1111"
25750 DATA  "     1"
25760 DATA  "    1"
25770 DATA  "111"
25780 DATA  "-1"
26500 DATA  5,7: REM  A
26510 DATA  "  1"
26520 DATA  " 1 1"
26530 DATA  "1    1"
26540 DATA  "1    1"
28550 DATA  "11111"
26560 DATA  "1    1"
26570 DATA  "1    1"
26580 DATA  "-1"
26600 DATA  5,7: REM  B
26610 DATA  "1111"
26620 DATA  "1    1"
26630 DATA  "1    1"
26640 DATA  "1111"
26650 DATA  "1    1"
26660 DATA  "1    1"
26670 DATA  "1111"
26680 DATA  "-1"
26700 DATA  5,7: REM  C
26710 DATA  " 111"
26720 DATA  "1    1"
26730 DATA  "1"
26740 DATA  "1"
26750 DATA  "1"
26760 DATA  "1    1"
26770 DATA  " 111"
26780 DATA  "-1"
26800 DATA  5,7: REM  D
26810 DATA  "1111"
26820 DATA  "1    1"
26830 DATA  "1    1"
26840 DATA  "1    1"
26850 DATA  "1    1"
26860 DATA  "1    1"
26870 DATA  "1111"
```

```
26880   DATA   "-1"
26900   DATA   5,7: REM   E
26910   DATA   "11111"
26920   DATA   "1"
26930   DATA   "1"
26940   DATA   "1111"
26950   DATA   "1"
26960   DATA   "1"
26970   DATA   "11111"
26980   DATA   "-1"
27000   DATA   5,7: REM   F
27010   DATA   "11111"
27020   DATA   "1"
27030   DATA   "1"
27040   DATA   "1111"
27050   DATA   "1"
27060   DATA   "1"
27070   DATA   "1"
27080   DATA   "-1"
27100   DATA   5,7: REM   G
27110   DATA   " 1111"
27120   DATA   "1"
27130   DATA   "1"
27140   DATA   "1"
27150   DATA   "1   11"
27160   DATA   "1    1"
27170   DATA   " 1111"
27180   DATA   "-1"
27200   DATA   5,7: REM   H
27210   DATA   "1    1"
27220   DATA   "1    1"
27230   DATA   "1    1"
27240   DATA   "11111"
27250   DATA   "1    1"
27260   DATA   "1    1"
27270   DATA   "1    1"
27280   DATA   "-1"
27300   DATA   3,7: REM   I
27310   DATA   "111"
27320   DATA   " 1"
27330   DATA   " 1"
27340   DATA   " 1"
27350   DATA   " 1"
27360   DATA   " 1"
27370   DATA   "111"
27380   DATA   "-1"
27400   DATA   6,7: REM   J
27410   DATA   "    111"
27420   DATA   "      1"
27430   DATA   "      1"
27440   DATA   "      1"
27450   DATA   "      1"
27460   DATA   "1     1"
27470   DATA   " 111"
27480   DATA   "-1"
27500   DATA   5,7: REM   K
27510   DATA   "1    1"
27520   DATA   "1   1"
27530   DATA   "1 1"
27540   DATA   "11"
27550   DATA   "1 1"
27560   DATA   "1   1"
27570   DATA   "1    1"
27580   DATA   "-1"
27600   DATA   4,7: REM   L
27610   DATA   "1"
27620   DATA   "1"
27630   DATA   "1"
27640   DATA   "1"
27650   DATA   "1"
27660   DATA   "1"
27670   DATA   "1111"
27680   DATA   "-1"
```

```
27700  DATA  7,7: REM  M
27710  DATA  "1        1"
27720  DATA  "11      11"
27730  DATA  "1 1  1 1"
27740  DATA  "1   1   1"
27750  DATA  "1       1"
27760  DATA  "1       1"
27770  DATA  "1       1"
27780  DATA  "-1"
27800  DATA  5,7: REM  N
27810  DATA  "1     1"
27820  DATA  "1     1"
27830  DATA  "11    1"
27840  DATA  "1 1 1"
27850  DATA  "1  11"
27860  DATA  "1   1"
27870  DATA  "1   1"
27880  DATA  "-1"
27900  DATA  5,7: REM  O
27910  DATA  " 111"
27920  DATA  "1   1"
27930  DATA  "1   1"
27940  DATA  "1   1"
27950  DATA  "1   1"
27960  DATA  "1   1"
27970  DATA  " 111"
27980  DATA  "-1"
28000  DATA  5,7: REM  P
28010  DATA  "1111"
28020  DATA  "1   1"
28030  DATA  "1   1"
28040  DATA  "1111"
28050  DATA  "1"
28060  DATA  "1"
28070  DATA  "1"
28080  DATA  "-1"
28100  DATA  5,7: REM  Q
28110  DATA  " 111"
28120  DATA  "1   1"
28130  DATA  "1   1"
28140  DATA  "1   1"
28150  DATA  "1 1 1"
28160  DATA  "1  1 "
28170  DATA  " 11 1"
28180  DATA  "-1"
28200  DATA  5,7: REM  R
28210  DATA  "1111"
28220  DATA  "1   1"
28230  DATA  "1   1"
28240  DATA  "1111"
28250  DATA  "1 1"
28260  DATA  "1  1"
28270  DATA  "1   1"
28280  DATA  "-1"
28300  DATA  5,7: REM  S
28310  DATA  " 111"
28320  DATA  "1   1"
28330  DATA  "1"
28340  DATA  " 111"
28350  DATA  "    1"
28360  DATA  "1   1"
28370  DATA  " 111"
28380  DATA  "-1"
28400  DATA  5,7: REM  T
28410  DATA  "11111"
28420  DATA  "  1"
28430  DATA  "  1"
28440  DATA  "  1"
28450  DATA  "  1"
28460  DATA  "  1"
28470  DATA  "  1"
28480  DATA  "-1"
28500  DATA  5,7: REM  U
```

```
28510   DATA   "1     1"
28520   DATA   "1     1"
28530   DATA   "1     1"
28540   DATA   "1     1"
28550   DATA   "1     1"
28560   DATA   "1     1"
28570   DATA   " 111"
28580   DATA   "-1"
28600   DATA   5,7:  REM   V
28610   DATA   "1     1"
28620   DATA   "1     1"
28630   DATA   "1     1"
28640   DATA   "1     1"
28650   DATA   "1     1"
28660   DATA   " 1   1 "
28670   DATA   "  1  "
28680   DATA   "-1"
28700   DATA   7,7:  REM   W
28710   DATA   "1       1"
28720   DATA   "1       1"
28730   DATA   "1       1"
28740   DATA   "1   1   1"
28750   DATA   "1 1 1 1"
28760   DATA   "11     11"
28770   DATA   "1       1"
28780   DATA   "-1"
28800   DATA   5,7:  REM   X
28810   DATA   "1     1"
28820   DATA   "1     1"
28830   DATA   " 1   1 "
28840   DATA   "  1  "
28850   DATA   " 1   1 "
28860   DATA   "1     1"
28870   DATA   "1     1"
28880   DATA   "-1"
28900   DATA   5,7:  REM   Y
28910   DATA   "1     1"
28920   DATA   "1     1"
28930   DATA   " 1   1 "
28940   DATA   "   1  "
28950   DATA   "   1  "
28960   DATA   "   1  "
28970   DATA   "   1  "
28980   DATA   "-1"
29000   DATA   5,7:  REM   Z
29010   DATA   "   1  "
29020   DATA   "11111"
29030   DATA   "      1"
29040   DATA   "     1"
29050   DATA   "   1  "
29060   DATA   "  1  "
29070   DATA   "1"
29080   DATA   "11111"
29090   DATA   "-1"
60000   :
60010   REM   * COPYRIGHT 1981 BY HOWARD FRANKLIN, PALO ALTO, CA *
60020   :
```

Type this routine and SAVE it as IMAGE MODULE.

Displaying Letters and Numbers

You must follow three steps to display a LO-RES image. First, specify the image to be displayed. Next, specify where it should be printed on the screen. Last, indicate the colors to be used.

IMAGE MODULE makes it very easy to display letters or numbers at different locations on the screen. You simply specify the contents of a string (X$), determine the distance from the top of the screen (XV), decide whether the string will be centered on the row, and choose the color (XC(1)). If you do not want the string centered, you must also specify where the string will start. Set XH, the distance from the left side of the screen.

The next section explains how the image gets colored. Remember those 1's you typed in the image DATA statements? We designed the letters and numerals so they can only be displayed in a single color. However, we did not indicate the color in the module. When you use an image, you specify its color by assigning one of the sixteen APPLE LO-RES colors to the 1's used in the DATA statements. For example, if you want the image to be light green, you would type XC(1) = 12. This assigns APPLE color 12 to the 1's which make up that image. If you want the image to be pink, you would type XC(1) = 11. Later in the chapter, you will see how to design and color images made with more than one color.

Following are some ways you can use IMAGE MODULE to display words. Add these statements to IMAGE MODULE and RUN it:

```
100 GR:HOME
110 X$ = "CAT"
120 XV = 10
130 XC(1) = 3
140 GOSUB 15300
999 END
```

Notice that the string is printed in green (line 130) and that the tops of the letters are in row 10 (line 120). The string "CAT" is centered because the IMAGE MODULE subroutine was entered at line 15300. Add the following lines and RUN the program again:

```
145 :
150 XH = 5
160 XV = 20
170 XC(1) = 8
180 GOSUB 15400
```

The added lines changed some of the variables. Since X$ was not changed, the screen displaying CAT was repeated. Try modifying this program so that your name is displayed in different colors and in different places on the screen. Watch what happens if you position the letters to overlap.

Be sure to specify all the string positioning information. When we entered the module at 15300, the string was centered; when we entered the module at 15400, it was not automatically centered. If you do not want to center the string, you must be sure to specify the starting position, XH (see line 150).d10GOLDEN DELICIOUS

1. What will be displayed when you merge IMAGE MODULE with the following program and RUN it?

```
100 GR:HOME
110 X$ = "CAT"
120 XV = 20
130 XC(1) = 3
140 GOSUB 15300
150 XC(1) = 13
160 GOSUB 15300
999 END
```

2. What will happen if we add 145 GR:HOME to the program?

— — — — — — — — — —

1. The word CAT will be displayed in purple. Then the same word, in the same position, will be colored yellow.
2. The screen will clear before the yellow word is displayed.

A neat addition available as part of IMAGE MODULE is a routine to wash the screen with the color of your choice. Add these lines to your current program and RUN it again:

```
102 COLOR = 5
104 GOSUB 15500
```

On some occasions you might get X$ from the keyboard instead of assigning it in the program. For example, you might want to ask for a name and then display it in large letters. The letters are large, however, and some names might not fit. The IMAGE MODULE subroutines check the string length and allow you to avoid truncating the name.

If you enter the routine at 15300 (for centering the display), the routine checks the length of the string and displays it only if it will all fit on the screen. If it will not fit, the routine displays nothing. If you enter the routine at 15400, however, the routine will truncate the string to fit on the screen.

IMAGE MODULE subroutines set the variable Z% upon exit, to indicate whether or not the images fit. If Z% equals 0, the images fit and are displayed; if Z% equals 1, the images do not fit and none are displayed (if 15300 is the entry point) or only the ones that fit are displayed (if 15400 is the entry point).

The following routine tests Z%. Add these lines to IMAGE MODULE:

```
100 GR:HOME
110 PRINT "PLEASE TYPE YOUR NICKNAME.";
120 INPUT X$
130 XV = 10: XC(1) = 3
140 GOSUB 15300
150 IF Z% = 0 GOTO 200
160 PRINT "THERE WERE TOO MANY LETTERS."
170 PRINT "PLEASE TRY AGAIN WITH FEWER."
180 GOTO 110
200: continue the program
```

RUN it.

Have you noticed that you have to wait a while for each letter to be displayed? It takes longer to display this kind of letter than a text letter (a letter in a program listing). The letters and numbers you see in text mode are created very quickly by the internal logic of the machine. The images presented here are created, piece by piece, by the logic of a BASIC program and, hence, take longer.

SUGGESTIONS FOR LETTER GAMES

Here are suggestions for two skill-building games you can design to help teach number recognition and keyboard familiarity to beginning readers.

In the first game, the player types a letter and the program displays it using the LO-RES images. An adult, sitting with a beginning learner, can say the names of the letters as they are displayed to reinforce the learning.

A second game displays a number and the player is asked to press the corresponding key. You might want to ignore all other keys to avoid confusion. When the player presses the correct key, the program makes a tone and presents another number.

UNDERSTANDING OUR
LINE-NUMBERING CONVENTIONS

Beginning in line 24800 of IMAGE MODULE are the DATA statements that contain the images. Look back at them and note the conventions we used in designing the images and assigning line numbers. Each image begins on a line number that is a multiple of 100; each image begins with a DATA statement containing its width and height and a REM telling which image it is; each image ends with a DATA "−1."

This particular line numbering convention allows us to access the images very easily, so it is important that you understand it. If you subtract 20000 from the line number of an image, you will see that the result is equal to 100 times the ASCII value of that character. For example, the A image begins at line 26500. 26500 minus 20000 is 6500, or 100 times the ASCII value for A. The ASCII value for B is 66. Notice that the DATA statements for B begin on line 26600.

Our line-numbering convention allows us to specify ASCII images using their character values, e.g., "A" for image number 65. This also means that you can create images for other keyboard characters and later access them in strings using their character values.

Later you might want to design lower-case letters to complement the upper-case ones we provide. We suggest numbering them starting at image 97 (line 29700) so that the lower-case image number equals the upper-case ASCII number, plus 32 (this means that you are using standard ASCII for lower case also.) When you want to refer to them in a string, add the following subroutine to IMAGE MODULE to convert upper-case ASCII to lower-case image numbers:

```
15591:
15592 REM * CONVERT UPPER CASE TO LOWER CASE *
15593 REM ENTRY: Z$ UPPER CASE
15594 REM EXIT: Z1$ LOWER CASE
15599:
15600 Z1$ = ""
15610 IF LEN(Z$) = 0 THEN RETURN:REM EMPTY
15620 FOR Z = 1 TO LEN(Z$)
15630 Z1$ = Z1$ + CHR$(ASC(MID$(Z$,Z,1)) + 32)
15640 NEXT
15650 RETURN
```

For example, if you added lower-case images to IMAGE MODULE, you could set X$ = "Cat" as follows:

```
500 Z$ = "AT":GOSUB 15600
510 X$ = "C" + Z1$
```

Our line-numbering conventions allow room for 255 images (lines 20100 through 45599). Reserving image numbers 32 through 127 for the ASCII characters, you will have room for many more of your own.

MAKING AN IMAGE LIBRARY

You would probably like to have many other images. We suggest you begin creating an image library of your own. Image numbers 1 through 31 and 128 through 255 are available to use within IMAGE MODULE. When you have written your program, you can merge IMAGE MODULE with it and have all the images available at once. To save space in a program, delete the images you don't want after you have merged IMAGE MODULE. By making an image library and using it this way, you can save and easily reuse the images you have spent time creating.

DESIGNING AND INCORPORATING NEW IMAGES

The easiest way to create images is to design them on graph paper and then copy the picture by typing numbers into DATA statements. Because the color dots on the screen are not perfectly square, however, the image on the screen will not be exactly the same shape as the one on the graph paper. A two-color tree designed on graph paper might look like Figure 1.

Modify IMAGE MODULE as follows:

```
10   REM   ...TWO COLOR TREE-IMAGE MODULE...
11 :
100  GR : HOME
110  X$ =  CHR$ (1)
120  XC(1) = 4
130  XC(2) = 8
140   GOSUB 15300
999  END
20100   DATA  21,38: REM   TWO-COLOR TREE
20102   DATA  "    11111111111111"
20104   DATA  "   111111111111111"
20106   DATA  "1111111111111111111"
20108   DATA  "1111111111111111111"
20110   DATA  "111111111111111111111"
20112   DATA  "111111111111111111111"
20114   DATA  "111111111111111111111"
20116   DATA  "111111111111111111111"
20118   DATA  "111111111111111111111"
20120   DATA  "111111111111111111111"
20122   DATA  "111111111111111111111"
20124   DATA  "111111111111111111111"
20126   DATA  "111111111111111111111"
20128   DATA  "1111111  2211111111111"
20130   DATA  "   11111  22  11111111"
20132   DATA  "   11111  22     11111"
20134   DATA  "    1111  22       11 "
20136   DATA  "          22"
20138   DATA  "          22"
20140   DATA  "          22"
20142   DATA  "          22"
20144   DATA  "          22"
20146   DATA  "          22"
20148   DATA  "          22"
20150   DATA  "          22"
20152   DATA  "          22"
20154   DATA  "          22"
20156   DATA  "          22"
20158   DATA  "          22"
20160   DATA  "          22"
20162   DATA  "          22"
20164   DATA  "          22"
20166   DATA  "          22"
20168   DATA  "          22"
20170   DATA  "          22"
20172   DATA  "          22"
20174   DATA  "          22"
20176   DATA  "        22222222 "
20178   DATA  "-1"
```

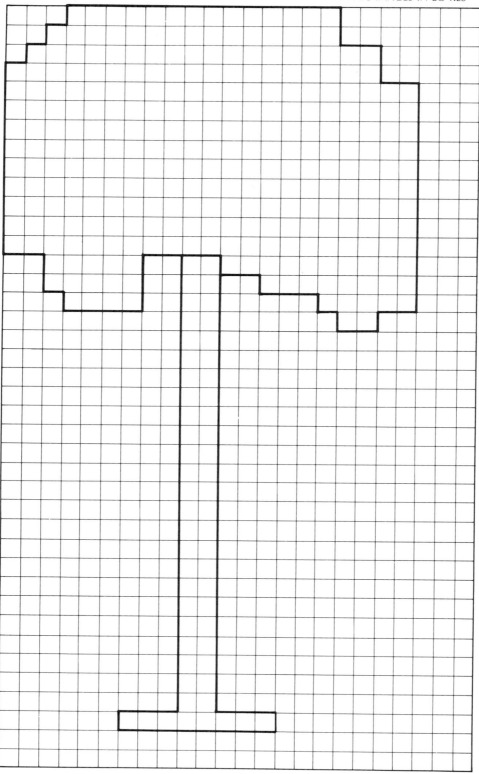

Note that lines 20100 through 20178 correspond to the graph. Type this and SAVE it as TWO-COLOR TREE. The TWO-COLOR TREE image number does not have an ASCII equivalent, so you access the image differently (see line 110). Instead of typing the string of characters in X$, type the reference to the image. For example, to access image number 130, use the statement X$ = CHR$(130). Using this method, you can position images the same way you position character strings. Assign the image number to X$ using CHR$; then enter the IMAGE MODULE at either 15300 or 15400.

You can also use X$ to position several images in a row. Write the assignments in the following form:

```
X$ = CHR$(130) + CHR$(140)
```

where 130 and 140 are image numbers.

Finally, a word about spacing the images in the X$. As the module is presently written, it creates one space between successive images. If you want to change it, set XS to the number of spaces you want before you enter the module (see lines 15310 and 15410).

REUSING AN IMAGE WITH DIFFERENT COLORS

When we created the image, we assigned a number to each of the blocks on the graph paper that we may want to color. The spaces (the blocks without numbers) do not get colored. Later, when we include the image in a program, we will translate each number into an APPLE color, just as we did with the 1's in the letter images.

We can have a dark green tree with a brown trunk by setting XC(1) = 4 and XC(2) = 8. Later we can use the same image and have a yellow tree with a white trunk by assigning XC(1) = 12 and XC(2) = 15. Still later we can have a red tree with a red trunk by typing XC(1) = 1 and XC(2) = 1.

Using this color-numbering method, you can design an image without immediately deciding which colors you are going to use. You can try different combinations of colors just by making different color assignments. This kind of flexibility is particularly useful when you are designing something like the next tree shown in Figure 2.

We used three numbers in this image. By assigning colors to the
numbers in different ways, we can make very different-looking
trees. Modify IMAGE MODULE as follows:

```
10   REM    ...THREE COLOR TREE-IMAGE MODULE...
11   :
100  GR : HOME
110  X$ = CHR$ (2)
120  XV = 0
130  XC(1) = 1
140  XC(2) = 2
150  XC(3) = 3
160  GOSUB 15300
170  PRINT : PRINT "PRESS ANY KEY TO CONTINUE... ";
180  GET Z$
200  GR : HOME
210  XV = 0
220  XC(1) = 3
230  XC(2) = 4
240  XC(3) = 5
250  GOSUB 15300
260  PRINT : PRINT "PRESS ANY KEY TO CONTINUE... ";
270  GET Z$
300  GR : HOME
310  XV = 0
320  XC(1) = 9
330  XC(2) = 9
340  XC(3) = 9
350  GOSUB 15300
360  PRINT : PRINT "PRESS ANY KEY TO CONTINUE... ";
370  GET Z$
400  GR : HOME
410  XV = 0
420  XC(1) = 5
430  XC(2) = 5
440  XC(3) = 6
450  GOSUB 15300
460  PRINT : PRINT "PRESS ANY KEY TO CONTINUE... ";
470  GET Z$
500  GR : HOME
510  XV = 0
520  XC(1) = 0
530  XC(2) = 0
540  XC(3) = 8
550  GOSUB 15300
999  END
20200 DATA   23,39: REM  THREE-COLOR TREE
20202 DATA   "   1111111111111111"
20204 DATA   "   1221111111111111"
20206 DATA   "11221111111111222111"
20208 DATA   "111111111111122221111"
20210 DATA   "111112221111111111111111"
20212 DATA   "131111112221111111131111"
20214 DATA   "131131111111111111322111"
20216 DATA   "133332211111111223111111"
20218 DATA   "111132223131111113111311"
20220 DATA   "121131111311112113133111"
20222 DATA   "  221311111312221313111111"
20224 DATA   "  133311121131111113322"
20226 DATA   "  111311222131313333  1"
20228 DATA   "  1113311111333"
20230 DATA   "        33111133"
20232 DATA   "         333333"
20234 DATA   "           33"
20236 DATA   "           33"
20238 DATA   "           33"
20240 DATA   "           33"
20242 DATA   "           33"
```

```
20244   DATA    "           33"
20246   DATA    "           33"
20248   DATA    "           33"
20250   DATA    "           33"
20252   DATA    "           33"
20254   DATA    "           33"
20256   DATA    "           33"
20258   DATA    "           33"
20260   DATA    "           33"
20262   DATA    "           33"
20264   DATA    "           33"
20266   DATA    "           33"
20268   DATA    "           33"
20270   DATA    "           33"
20272   DATA    "           33"
20274   DATA    "           33"
20276   DATA    "           33"
20278   DATA    "    3333333333"
20280   DATA    "-1"
```

Type it and SAVE it as THREE-COLOR TREE. Notice how the same image can look different depending on the color assignment (see lines 130 through 150, 220 through 240, 320 through 340, 420 through 440, and 520 through 540).

When we designed the tree, we decided which areas might have different colors and assigned a different number to each. (The more numbers you assign, the greater the flexibility you will have when you color the image.) Then, when we used the image in the program, we assigned different colors to the numbers. (One time we assigned the same color to several numbers—see lines 320 through 340, 420 through 440, and 520 through 540.) Using this method, you can design for a maximum of nine colors. Later you can control the "busyness" of the image with the actual color assignment statements. And, of course, you can use the image again another time with different color assignments.

The last image is even more complex and versatile. We used nine different numbers to designate different portions of this figure. Using different sets of colors, you can have four realistic arm-position combinations and four realistic leg-position combinations (Figure 3). (Assign black to the extra body parts.)

Make the following changes to IMAGE MODULE.

```
10   REM   ...PERSON-IMAGE MODULE...
11   :
100  C = 3: REM   # OF COLORINGS
110  FOR N = 1 TO C
120  X$ = CHR$ (3)
197  :
198  REM   * COLORS FOR N-TH PERSON AT LINE 500+10*N *
199  :
200  Z = 500 + 10 * N
210  GOSUB 19000
220  FOR J = 1 TO 9
230  READ XC(J)
240  NEXT
300  GR : HOME
310  XV = 0
320  GOSUB 15300
400  PRINT
410  PRINT "PRESS RETURN TO CONTINUE... ";
420  GET Z$
430  NEXT
490  END
497  REM   * VALUES FOR XC(1),...,XC(9) *
498  REM   (N-TH PERSON COLORS AT LINE 500+10*N)
499  .
510  DATA   5,0,0,5,5,0,5,0,5
520  DATA   1,0,1,0,1,0,1,0,1
530  DATA   0,4,4,0,4,4,0,4,0
20300 DATA   20,39: REM   PERSON
20302 DATA   "        555      333"
20304 DATA   "        555        3"
20306 DATA   "        555        3"
20308 DATA   "        555        3"
20310 DATA   "        555        3"
20312 DATA   "          5        3"
20314 DATA   "          5        3"
20316 DATA   "    22222555555533333"
20318 DATA   "    2   1155555 4"
20320 DATA   "    2  11 55555 4"
20322 DATA   "    2 11   55555 4"
20324 DATA   "    211    55555 4    4"
20326 DATA   "    21     55555 4    4"
20328 DATA   "    21     55555 444444"
20330 DATA   "22211      55555"
20332 DATA   "      11   55555"
20334 DATA   "       11155555"
20336 DATA   "        1155555"
20338 DATA   "  777777755555"
20340 DATA   "  777777755555"
20342 DATA   "  77       88 55"
20344 DATA   "  77       88 55"
20346 DATA   "  77       88 55"
20348 DATA   "  77       88 55"
20350 DATA   "  77       88 55"
20352 DATA   "  77       88 55"
20354 DATA   "  77       88 559999999"
20356 DATA   "777        88 559999999"
20358 DATA   "777        88 66     99"
20360 DATA   "           88 66     99"
20362 DATA   "           88 66     99"
20364 DATA   "           88 66"
20366 DATA   "           88 66"
20368 DATA   "           88 66"
20370 DATA   "           88 66"
20372 DATA   "           88 66"
20374 DATA   "           88 66"
20376 DATA   "      88888 66666"
20378 DATA   "      88888 66666"
20380 DATA   "-1"
```

RUN it.

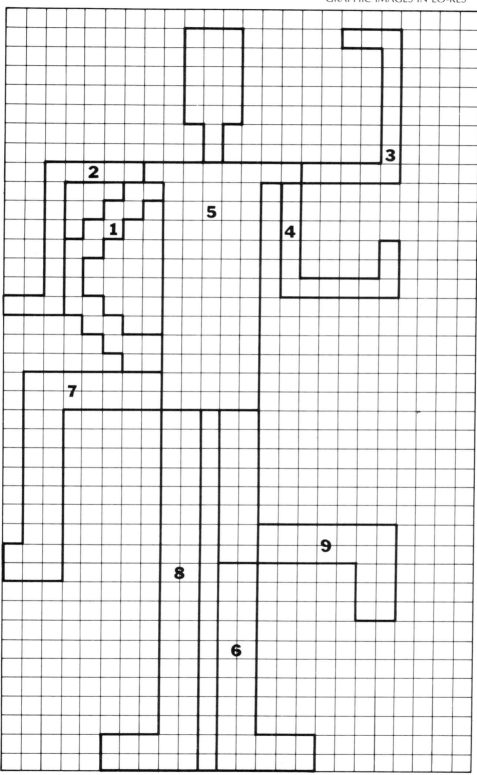

To show one hand on hip and one arm in the air, color 1, 3, and 5 the same, and assign black to 2 and 4. How would you place the arms so the figure looks like an Egyptian drawing?

To make the figure stand up straight, color 5, 6, and 8 the same and assign black to 7 and 9. Can you color the figure so only the left leg is raised?

DIFFERENT TV, DIFFERENT COLORS

In the last chapter, you played with colors when you made the boxes and borders. Now that you are making images, you may want to take the colors more seriously. The colors you see on your screen depend on your particular TV set. In fact, your program may look different when it's being displayed on a different TV. APPLE supplies a color testing chart you can use to see what the colors look like. Look for it in your *APPLESOFT Reference Manual.*

We strongly encourage you to make your own images. It's really fun, and it will help make your programs uniquely your own. You can make big images that simply appear during a program. Or you can make little images and move them around on the screen. The important thing to remember, though, is that they are stored in DATA statements, so you cannot use the same line numbers for different images.

CHAPTER SUMMARY

This chapter showed how to use IMAGE MODULE to create LO-RES graphic letters and numerals and also how to design and use original images. You will find IMAGE MODULE very useful when you are writing your own game programs. Later in the book you will see how we used it in the games we wrote.

CHAPTER FOUR

High-Resolution Graphics

In this chapter you will learn a little bit about how to use the high-resolution graphics capability of the APPLE II. High-resolution (HI-RES) graphics are much more complicated to use than LO-RES. As a matter of fact, they are so complicated that we are not going to show you all the details. We have discovered that very few things can be done in HI-RES from APPLESOFT BASIC without an enormous amount of detailed programming. Many game-type programs feature HI-RES graphics that use machine language subroutines to greatly speed up the display process. However, since the subroutines are not done in BASIC and since machine language programming is beyond the scope of this book, we will only remind you that the programs are probably much more complex than they look at first. Another way of thinking about HI-RES programming is, "What you've seen, you can't do!"

The APPLE designers attempted to resolve some of the difficulty of doing HI-RES graphics in BASIC by introducing the concept of using shape tables. Shape tables allow you to design, create, and manipulate shapes using a special set of instructions. Unfortunately, even shape tables are slow, cumbersome, difficult to use, and too intricate to discuss in this book. For example, they are inadequate to create a HI-RES map of the United States.

For those of you who want more details on HI-RES graphics shape tables, we suggest Chapter 9 of the *APPLESOFT Reference Manual* that came with your computer. We also suggest that you consider purchasing any one of the several well-documented, high-resolution graphics software packages that are currently available. Using a commercial package is much easier than trying to figure out how to do HI-RES in BASIC. Check your local computer store for their favorite package. Then look carefully at the documentation to be sure you understand how to use it.

FUNDAMENTALS OF HI-RES

Now that you know what you can't do in BASIC, we'll show you some things you can do. HI-RES graphics uses two graphics screens, screen one and screen two. To use screen one, use the instruction HGR. HGR2 tells your program to use screen two. Either of these two instructions clears the appropriate graphic screen to black. Screen one can display a matrix of 280 dots across (0 through 279) and 160 dots down (0 through 159). "Beneath" HI-RES screen one is blank screen space on which you can display four lines of regular text, using normal PRINT statements in your BASIC program. Screen two displays a matrix of 280 by 192 dots with no text space.

The instruction HCOLOR tells the program which HI-RES color to use when plotting on the HI-RES screens. The eight HI-RES colors available and their color numbers are shown below:

0 = black	4 = black
1 = green	5 = orange
2 = violet	6 = blue
3 = white	7 = white

Note the duplication of black and white colors (the reason for the duplication is quite technical). You should also note that colors 5 and 6 may not appear as orange and blue on your TV screen. One of the difficulties with HI-RES color is the tremendous variation among home television sets. The colors in our program may depend on the set you show them on. To avoid some of the problems, you can stick with black and white graphics!

To select white as your plotting color, use this instruction:

HCOLOR = 3

White will be plotted on the screen until another HCOLOR statement is executed changing the plot color.

The HPLOT instruction is used to plot a point or a line on the HI-RES screen. The upper left corner of the screen is considered position 0, 0. All points are plotted in relation to this point.

HPLOT 25, 55 will plot a point in the current color located at the dot 25 columns over and 55 rows down from the upper-left corner of the screen.

HPLOT 10,20 to 110,90 will plot a diagonal line from point 10, 20 to point 110, 90.

To continue the plot line from point 110, 90, use this abbreviated form of HPLOT:

HPLOT TO 160, 20

This abbreviated form of the HPLOT statement assumes that you want to continue plotting from the last point plotted (in our case 110, 90).

You could combine the above into one HPLOT statement that looks like this:

HPLOT 10,20 TO 110,90 to 160, 20

The following program is a demonstration of the HI-RES commands you have learned so far.

```
10   REM   ...HI-RES DEMO1...
11   :
110  HGR
120  HCOLOR= 3
130  HPLOT 25,55
140  GOSUB 220
150  HPLOT 10,20 TO 110,90
160  GOSUB 220
170  HPLOT  TO 160,20
180  GOSUB 220
190  GOTO 300
215  :
220  PRINT "PRESS RETURN TO CONTINUE:";
230  INPUT R$
240  RETURN
300  END
```

Enter it and RUN it.

1.   Write the statement that will cause the plot line to continue down the screen in a straight line to position 90.

185

2.   Write a statement that will change the plot color to green. Then write another statement to plot a horizontal line across the entire screen and just below the plot line now on the screen.

190
200

— — — — — — — — — —

1.   185 HPLOT TO 160,90
2.   190 HCOLOR = 1
      200 HPLOT 0, 90 to 279, 90

To wash the screen with a color background instead of the black background that is cleared by HGR and HGR2, use this procedure:
—HGR or HGR2
—POKE 28, X
—CALL 62454
X can be any color from 0 through 255. Except for the values indicated below, you will get an interesting striped color image on your screen. These values of X in the POKE statement will give you a solid background in the color indicated:

black—0 or 128
white—127 or 255
green—42
violet—85
orange—170
blue—213

The screen wash works very quickly. Once the screen color is established, you can plot lines in other colors over the background color.

SOME HI-RES PROBLEMS

The program you tried earlier worked just as you might have expected. You can even change the colors and the program will still work. When you switch to screen two by using HGR2, the program will also work, except for the "press RETURN" prompts. They will not appear because screen two has no text window.

We make a point of mentioning that this program works as you would expect because, as a result of variations in televisions as well as pecularities in HI-RES, things do not always work as you might expect. Following is a classic example. The program below attempts to place a nice single-color border around HI-RES screen one. Enter the program and RUN it to see what happens.

```
10    REM    ...HIRES BORDER...
11    :
12    REM    BORDER DEMO IN EACH COLOR
13    :
100   FOR J = 0 TO 7: REM   USE EACH COLOR
110   HOME : HGR
120   HCOLOR= J: REM   NEXT COLOR
200   HPLOT 0,0 TO 279,0 TO 279,159 TO 0,159 TO 0,0
300   VTAB 22: PRINT "BORDER IN COLOR ";J
310   PRINT
320   PRINT "PRESS RETURN FOR THE NEXT COLOR... ";
330   GET Z$
340   IF Z$ = CHR$ (27) THEN   TEXT : END : REM   ESC
350   NEXT
360   GOTO 100: REM   LOOP
```

As you can see, some of the borders were incomplete and some of them appeared with multiple colors. How do things like that happen? There is no easy answer to that question.

1.   Why did nothing appear on the screen for colors 0 and 4?

2.   Which colors displayed a complete four-sided border, though colors may have been mixed?

— — — — — — — — —

1.   Those are black colors that are not visible and did not appear on the black screen.
2.   Colors 3 and 7 are white and did display four sides of the border, though the vertical sides were odd colors on our TV.

Now add this statement to your program and RUN it again to observe the change:

       210 HPLOT 1,1 TO 278,1 TO 278, 158 TO 1, 158 TO 1, 1

The purpose of this statement is to make a double border around the screen (an inner border) to see if that improves our picture.
Which colors now have a full, normal, one-color border?

— — — — — — — — —

Green, violet, white, and blue were normal. On our screen, color 5 (orange) had two or more colors and color 7 (white) did not appear correctly. Much to our surprise, the same problem appeared when we ran this program using an expensive video monitor.
   Now delete statement 200 in your program to see if a single inner-border will appear correctly.
What happens when you RUN the program now?

— — — — — — — — —

The odd color problems reappeared just as they did when we first ran the program.

These same problems appear when you use HI-RES screen two. Type this little program and RUN it:

```
100 HGR
110 HCOLOR = 1
120 HPLOT 50,0 TO 70, 150
```

You would expect a single line to be plotted on the screen. What actually appeared on the screen?

_____ _____ _____ _____ _____

A series of short plot lines from point to point appeared, rather than one continuous line.

Change the color to see if that changes the image. Try changing the plot line points. Your screen image will change in an interesting manner.

Other problems may also appear on a HI-RES screen. Some are called clutter, others artifacts. One common problem is the unwanted orange stripe that sometimes displays down the left side of the screen. It is a function of what appears to be an error in the HI-RES graphic software. Other problems are not a function of your APPLE or the HI-RES capability of the APPLE. Rather, they are a product of the circuitry found in television sets and more expensive color video monitors.

FUN WITH HI-RES

This chapter could not end without some examples of what can be done quickly and easily with HI-RES graphics. (You really can do things!) But don't expect perfection. As you try these exercises, you will see color imperfections appear on your screen. Don't fret . . . that's just HI-RES!

Enter and RUN this program that displays a simple string pattern in HI-RES graphics.

```
10   REM   ...STRING PATTERN...
11 :
12   REM   SIMPLE STRING PATTERN
13 :
100   TEXT : REM   FORCE FULL SCREEN
110 HO = 0: REM   H-ORIGIN
120 VO = 159: REM   V-ORIGIN
130 MS = 19: REM   MAXIMUM STEP SIZE
200   HOME : HGR
210 S% = MS *  RND (1) + 1: REM   SELECT RANDOM STEP SIZE
220   HTAB 1: VTAB 22: PRINT "STEP SIZE = ";S%
230 Z% = 7 *  RND (1) + 1: IF Z% = 4 THEN 230: REM   SELECT RANDOM
     NON-BLACK COLOR
240   HCOLOR= Z%
300 R% = VO / S% * S%: REM   RANGE
310   FOR J = 0 TO R% STEP S%: REM   STEP THROUGH ENDPOINTS IN THE RANGE
320   HPLOT HO,VO - R% + J TO HO + J,VO: REM   NEXT STRING SEGMENT
390   NEXT
500   PRINT
510   PRINT "PRESS RETURN FOR NEXT PATTERN... ";
520   GET Z$
530   IF Z$ =  CHR$ (27) THEN  TEXT : END : REM   ESC
540   GOTO 200
```

SAVE it using the name STRING PATTERN.

Here is a fancier version of a geometric string pattern. Geometric patterns are easy to reproduce in HI-RES and appear very clearly on the screen. This particular one is complex enough to cause color artifacts to appear on the screen in some of the displays. Make these changes to STRING PATTERN and SAVE it using the name STRING PATTERN2. RUN the program to see what it does. You might want to merge either of these two programs to your game programs to offer an interesting "time-out" or reward at the end of play.

```
10   REM   ...STRING2 PATTERN-STRING PATTERN
11 :
12   REM   FANCIER STRING PATTERN
13 .
110 HO = 139: REM   H-ORIGIN
120 VO = 79: REM   V-ORIGIN
130 MS = 11: REM   MAXIMUM STEP SIZE
330   HPLOT  TO HO,VO + R% - J: REM   LOWER RIGHT
340   HPLOT  TO HO - J,VO: REM   LOWER LEFT
350   HPLOT  TO HO,VO - R% + J: REM   UPPDR LEFT
```

CHAPTER SUMMARY

This chapter may be a disappointment to those of you who thought you might learn all there is to know about HI-RES graphics in just a few short pages. It is our feeling that HI-RES programming is simply beyond the scope of what can be expected of the average home/ school BASIC programmer. You will enjoy programming with HI-RES graphics much more if you purchase and use one of the many commercial software packages that take the pain out of HI-RES programming. Also, keep in mind that LO-RES programming is much easier to do and young children find LO-RES images just as enjoyable as HI-RES images.

CHAPTER FIVE

Routines for Entering Data

The object of this chapter is to show you how to use special data entry subroutines designed for your game programs. They are: The General-Purpose Input Subroutine, The Input Number Subroutine, The Y/N Subroutine, The Single-Character Input Subroutine, The Pause or Keystroke Subroutine, and the Get One Keystroke Without Echo Subroutine. Parts of this chapter are more technical than other chapters of this book because some of you may want to know some of the details of the data entry subroutines. If you don't want all the technical information, just read the "How to Use" sections to learn to use the six data entry routines.

One principal frustration experienced by computer game players is having a program terminate or "abort" in the middle of play because they entered incorrect data. Conversely, a chief frustration of computer game programmers is that inexperienced players will enter incorrect data or hit the wrong keys when entering data. This causes the program to abort or "blow-up," to the consternation of both player and programmer. The ultimate program includes data entry handlers, or routines, to test all data entered for validity and to then respond appropriately without allowing the program to terminate. A good data entry routine is designed with the novice player in mind and will usually accept only the intended keystrokes, essentially deactivating the rest of the keyboard. We have developed four data entry subroutines fitting that description. A fifth and sixth are offered that you may want to use for special purposes.

Here is the complete INPUT MODULE that contains all the sub-routines.

```
10   REM   ...INPUT MODULE...
11   :
12   REM   INPUT SUBROUTINES
13   :
9990 :
9991 :
9992 REM  ** INPUT AND ECHO A STRING ENDING WITH RETURN **
9993 REM  ENTRY: CURSOR SET TO BEGINNING OF INPUT FIELD
9994 REM            YW    FIELD WIDTH
9995 REM            YF$   FIELD FILLER CHARACTER
9996 REM  EXIT:     Z$    STRING
9997 REM            Z%    -1 (ESC); 0 (NOT ESC)
9999 :
10000 IF  LEN (YF$) <  > 1 THEN YF$ = " ": REM  INITIALIZE FILLER
     CHARACTER IF NECESSARY
10010 YH% = PEEK (36) + 1: REM  H-POS
10020 YV% = PEEK (37) + 1: REM  V-POS
10100 GOSUB 10500: REM  SET INPUT FIELD TO THE FILLER CHARACTER AND
     INITIALIZE
10110 GET Z1$
10120 IF Z1$ = CHR$ (13) THEN  RETURN : REM  RETURN
10130 IF Z1$ <  > CHR$ (27) THEN 10200: REM  ESC
10140 GOSUB 10500
10150 FLASH : PRINT "ESC"; CHR$ (8);: NORMAL
10160 Z% =  - 1: REM  ESC FLAG
10170 GOTO 10110
10200 IF Z1$ <  > CHR$ (8) THEN 10300: REM  LEFT ARROW
10210 IF Z% =  - 1 OR LEN (Z$) <  = 1 THEN 10100: REM  ESC AND ONE
     CHARACTER OR LESS SHARE LOGIC
10220 PRINT  CHR$ (8);YF$; CHR$ (8);: REM  ERASE ONE CHARACTER
10230 Z$ = LEFT$ (Z$, LEN (Z$) - 1)
10240 GOTO 10110 .
10300 IF Z1$ < " " THEN 10110: REM  IGNORE OTHER CONTROL CHARACTERS
10310 IF Z% =  - 1 THEN  GOSUB 10500: REM  CLEAR ESCAPE CONDITION
10320 IF  LEN (Z$) < YW THEN 10400
10330 IF YW = 0 THEN 10110: REM  DO NOT ECHO IF WIDTH=0
10340 PRINT  CHR$ (8);: REM  ALREADY AT MAX WIDTH
10350 IF  LEN (Z$) = 1 THEN Z$ = ""
10360 IF  LEN (Z$) > 1 THEN Z$ =  LEFT$ (Z$, LEN (Z$) - 1)
10400 PRINT Z1$;: REM  ECHO AND APPEND CHARACTER
10410 Z$ = Z$ + Z1$
10420 GOTO 10110
10500 HTAB YH%: VTAB YV%: FOR Z = 1 TO YW: PRINT YF$;: NEXT : REM
     SET FIELD TO FILLER CHARACTER
10510 PRINT " ";: REM  AND ERASE POSSIBLE CURSOR
10520 IF YW < 2 THEN  FOR Z = YW + 1 TO 3: PRINT " ";: NEXT : REM
     ERASE POSSIBLE ESC IF FIELD NOT WIDE ENOUGH
10530 HTAB YH%: VTAB YV%
10540 Z$ = ""
10550 Z% = 0
10560 RETURN
10591 :
10592 REM  * INPUT NUMBER *
10593 REM  ENTRY: CONDITIONS FOR INPUT STRING SET
10594 REM  EXIT:  Z% -1 (ESC); 0 (INVALID); 1 (INTEGER); 2 (DECIMAL)
10595 REM         Z VALUE (IF VALID)
10599 :
10600 GOSUB 10000: REM  GET STRING
10610 IF Z% =  - 1 OR  LEN (Z$) = 0 THEN  RETURN : REM  ESC OR RETURN
     ONLY (Z%=0)
10620 Z% = 1: REM  SET VALID FLAG
10630 FOR Z1 = 1 TO  LEN (Z$):Z1$ =  MID$ (Z$,Z1,1)
10640 IF Z1$ = "." AND Z% = 1 THEN Z% = 2: GOTO 10660: REM  TRAP FOR
     FIRST DECIMAL POINT
10650 IF (Z1$ < "0" OR Z1$ > "9") AND (Z1$ <  > "-" AND Z1 > 1) THEN
     Z% = 0: REM  INVALID IF NOT A DIGIT AND NOT A LEADING -
10660 NEXT
10670 Z = VAL (Z$): REM  VALUE ONLY IF VALID FLAG (Z%=1 OR 2)
10680 RETURN
```

```
10991 :
10992   REM   ** INPUT INTEGER **
10993   REM   ENTRY: CONDITIONS FOR INPUT STRING SET
10994   REM           YL   MINIMUM INTEGER
10995   REM           YH   MAXIMUM
10996   REM   EXIT:   Z%  -1 (ESC); 0 (INVALID INTEGER); 1 (VALID
        INTEGER)
10997   REM           Z    VALUE (IF INTEGER VALID)
10999 :
11000   GOSUB 10600: REM  INPUT NUMBER
11010   IF Z% < 1 THEN  RETURN : REM  ESC OR INVALID
11020   IF Z% = 2 THEN Z% = 0: RETURN : REM  INVALID IF DECIMAL POINT
11030   IF Z < YL OR Z > YH THEN Z% = 0: REM  INVALID IF OUT OF RANGE
11040   RETURN
11091 :
11092   REM   ** INPUT DECIMAL **
11093   REM   ENTRY: CONDITIONS FOR INPUT STRING SET
11094   REM           YL   MINIMUM VALUE
11095   REM           YH   MAXIMUM
11096   REM   EXIT:   Z%  -1 (ESC); 0 (INVALID); 1 (INTEGER); 2
        (DECIMAL)
11097   REM           Z    VALUE (IF VALID)
11099 :
11100   GOSUB 10600: REM  INPUT NUMBER
11110   IF Z% < 1 THEN  RETURN : REM  ESC OR INVALID
11120   IF Z < YL OR Z > YH THEN Z% = 0: REM  INVALID IF OUT OF RANGE
11130   RETURN
11191 :
11192   REM   ** INPUT Y OR N **
11193   REM   ENTRY: CURSOR AND FILLER CHARACTER SET
11194   REM   EXIT:   Z%  -1 (ESC); 0 (NEITHER Y NOR N); 1 (Y), 2 (N)
11199 :
11200   Y$ = "YN": REM  USE INPUT SINGLE CHARACTER ROUTINE
11291 :
11292   REM   ** INPUT SINGLE CHARACTER AND MATCH WITH VALID STRING **
11293   REM   ENTRY: CURSOR AND FILLER CHARACTER SET
11294   REM           Y$  STRING OF MATCH CHARACTERS
11295   REM   EXIT:   Z%  -1 (ESC); 0 (CHARACTER NOT IN STRING); J (J-TH
        CHARACTER IN MATCH STRING)
11299 :
11300   YW = 1: REM  SET FIELD WIDTH
11310   GOSUB 10000
11320   IF Z% = - 1 OR LEN (Z$) = 0 THEN  RETURN : REM  ESC OR
        RETURN ONLY (Z%=0)
11330   Z% = 0: REM  SET NOT MATCHED FLAG
11340   FOR Z1 = 1 TO  LEN (Y$)
11350   IF Z$ =  MID$ (Y$,Z1,1) THEN Z% = Z1: REM  MATCH IN POSITION
        Z1
11360   NEXT
11370   RETURN
11391 :
11392   REM   ** PAUSE OR UNTIL KEYSTROKE **
11393   REM   ENTRY: YP  LENGTH OF PAUSE IN INTERNAL TIME UNITS
11394   REM           0  WAIT FOR KEYSTROKE ONLY
11395   REM   EXIT:   Z%  -1 (ESC); 0 (PAUSE EXPIRED); 1 (KEYSTROKE
        BEFORE PAUSE EXPIRED)
11396   REM           Z    KEYSTROKE (ASCII VALUE + 128)
11399 :
11400   POKE  - 16368,0: REM  CLEAR TYPE-AHEAD
11410   Z1 = 0: REM  INITIALIZE COUNT (* ENTRY FOR GET ONE KEY *)
11420   Z1 = Z1 + 1
11430   Z =  PEEK ( - 16384)
11440   IF Z >  = 128 THEN Z% = 1 - 2 * (Z = 155): RETURN : REM
        KEYSTROKE; TRAP FOR ESC THEN RETURN
11450   IF Z1 < YP OR YP = 0 THEN 11420
11460   Z% = 0: REM  PAUSE EXPIRED
11470   RETURN
11491 :
11492   REM   ** GET ONE KEY, NO ECHO, NO TYPE-AHEAD **
11493   REM   EXIT: Z%  -1 (ESC); 1 (OTHER KEY)
11494   REM           Z    KEYSTROKE (ASCII VALUE + 128)
11499 :
11500   YP = 0: GOSUB 11400: REM  WAIT FOR KEYSTROKE
11510   POKE  - 16368,0: RETURN : REM  CLEAR KEYBOARD AND RETURN
11591 :
```

```
11592  REM  ** GET ONE KEY, NO ECHO, WITH TYPE-AHEAD **
11593  REM  EXIT: Z%  -1 (ESC); 1 (OTHER KEY)
11594  REM       Z   KEYSTROKE (ASCII VALUE + 128)
11599  :
11600  YP = 0: GOSUB 11420: REM  GET ONE KEY, NO TYPE-AHEAD
11610  POKE  - 16368,0: RETURN : REM  CLEAR KEYBOARD AND RETURN
60000  :
60010  REM  * COPYRIGHT 1981 BY HOWARD FRANKLIN, PALO ALTO, CA *
60020  :
```

Type it. Save it as INPUT MODULE.

GENERAL-PURPOSE INPUT SUBROUTINE

The General-Purpose Input Subroutine will accept any characters on the keyboard: numbers, letters, and special characters. It can be used for all data entry. However, by itself, we use it for entering only letters and special characters. The subroutine simulates the use of the normal BASIC INPUT statement. It requires that the user always press RETURN to indicate that the entry is complete. Some programmers mix GET and INPUT statements in the same program when asking for data. Novice users find it very confusing to PRESS RETURN for some answers and not press RETURN for others. Our data entry convention requires that the user always press RETURN. (Technical note: A GET statement is actually used for data entry, but each entry is tested for RETURN before the routine is terminated.)

Another programming convention introduced allows the user to press ESCAPE (ESC) at any time during entry, and tests for it. The ESC key assumes a special purpose, usually to signal that the user wants to end the play, and is tested by the General-Purpose Input Subroutine. If the user presses ESC, the word ESC flashes on the screen advising the user that ESC was pressed. Pressing RETURN ends the entry sequence signaling ESCape has been pressed. Pressing any other key before RETURN erases the ESC, and the program remains in the entry sequence. How the program itself responds to ESC will depend on what you, the programmer, tell it to do.

How to Use the General-Purpose Input Subroutine

The General-Purpose Input Subroutine starts at line 10000. Here are the REMark lines that precede the subroutine:

```
9990 :
9991 :
9992 REM ** INPUT AND ECHO A STRING ENDING WITH RETURN **
9993 REM ENTRY: CURSOR SET TO BEGINNING OF INPUT FIELD
9994 REM        YW    FIELD WIDTH
9995 REM        YF$   FIELD FILLER .CHARACTER
9996 REM EXIT:  Z$    STRING
9997 REM        Z%    -1 (ESC); 0 (NOT ESC)
9999 :
```

As you can see, there are entry variables, YW and YF$, and exit variables, Z$ and Z%. The entry variables must be defined before you enter the subroutine using GOSUB 10000. The YW variable determines the field width or number of characters that the subroutine will accept. If you want the user to enter a twenty-character name, then place this statement in the program:

```
200 YW = 20
```

YF$ is a filler character. It is most commonly used in games where the player makes guesses that fill in the blanks. If you do nothing to YF$, then the program assumes that YF$ contains a blank character and will display blanks on the screen where the user is entering characters. If you want the user to "fill-in" places, for example, indicating how many characters are acceptable, place some character into YF$. Here is an example:

```
210 YF$ = "-"
```

To use the subroutine in a game program, your program might look like this, where the field width is set to three and the filler character to "x":

```
200 YW = 3: YF$ = "x"
210 PRINT "ENTER A THREE DIGIT NUMBER: ";
220 GOSUB 10000
```

Write the BASIC statements that set the entry variables for a ten-character entry variable word. Use the equals sign as a filler character.

— — — — — — — — —

```
200 YW = 10: YF$ = "="
210 PRINT "ENTER A 10 CHAR WORD: ";
220 GOSUB 10000
```

The exit variables serve two functions. Z$ will contain the data that was entered and accepted, numbers or letters. Variable Z% will be set to −1 if the ESC was pressed or will remain at zero (0) if there was no escape. You can use the ESC key for many different purposes. This subroutine allows you the flexibility to choose how to use it. For some of our programs, we have adopted the convention that when the user presses ESC during play, it is a signal for "help," and the instructions or a note or clue of some kind are printed on the screen. If the user presses ESC again from the "help" screen, the program ends. To continue play from the "help" screen, the user could press RETURN. This is all controlled by using the INPUT MODULE's flexibility.

ESC can also be used to return to a menu of choices, to reshuffle cards in a card game, to quit the round but continue the game, and a host of other purposes. Using this subroutine, ESC is only detected. You, the programmer, determine what the program will do.

Here is the rest of the General-Purpose Input Subroutine.

```
10000   IF  LEN (YF$) <  > 1 THEN YF$ = " ": REM  INITIALIZE FILLER
        CHARACTER IF NECESSARY
10010 YH% =  PEEK (36) + 1: REM  H-POS
10020 YV% =  PEEK (37) + 1: REM  V-POS
10100   GOSUB 10500: REM  SET INPUT FIELD TO THE FILLER CHARACTER AND
        INITIALIZE
10110   GET Z1$
10120   IF Z1$ =  CHR$ (13) THEN  RETURN : REM  RETURN
10130   IF Z1$ <  >  CHR$ (27) THEN 10200: REM  ESC
10140   GOSUB 10500
10150   FLASH : PRINT "ESC"; CHR$ (8);: NORMAL
10160 Z% =  - 1: REM  ESC FLAG
10170   GOTO 10110
10200   IF Z1$ <  >  CHR$ (8) THEN 10300: REM  LEFT ARROW
10210   IF Z% =  - 1 OR  LEN (Z$) <  = 1 THEN 10100: REM  ESC AND ONE
        CHARACTER OR LESS SHARE LOGIC
10220   PRINT  CHR$ (8);YF$; CHR$ (8);: REM  ERASE ONE CHARACTER
10230 Z$ =  LEFT$ (Z$, LEN (Z$) - 1)
10240   GOTO 10110
10300   IF Z1$ <  " " THEN 10110: REM  IGNORE OTHER CONTROL CHARACTERS
10310   IF Z% =  - 1 THEN  GOSUB 10500: REM  CLEAR ESCAPE CONDITION
10320   IF  LEN (Z$) < YW THEN 10400
10330   IF YW = 0 THEN 10110: REM  DO NOT ECHO IF WIDTH=0
10340   PRINT  CHR$ (8);: REM  ALREADY AT MAX WIDTH
10350   IF  LEN (Z$) = 1 THEN Z$ = ""
10360   IF  LEN (Z$) > 1 THEN Z$ =  LEFT$ (Z$, LEN (Z$) - 1)
10400   PRINT Z1$;: REM  ECHO AND APPEND CHARACTER
10410 Z$ = Z$ + Z1$
10420   GOTO 10110
10500   HTAB YH%: VTAB YV%: FOR Z = 1 TO YW: PRINT YF$;: NEXT : REM
        SET FIELD TO FILLER CHARACTER
10510   PRINT " ";: REM  AND ERASE POSSIBLE CURSOR
10520   IF YW < 2 THEN  FOR Z = YW + 1 TO 3: PRINT " ";: NEXT : REM
        ERASE POSSIBLE ESC IF FIELD NOT WIDE ENOUGH
10530   HTAB YH%: VTAB YV%
10540 Z$ = ""
10550 Z% = 0
10560   RETURN
```

Note that all entered data are placed in a string variable (Z$).
Write the statements that will allow the user to enter a four-character
word, with the filler character being periods (.). Test for ESC (GOTO
4000). If no ESC, let the user enter another word with as many as ten
characters into a period-filled field.

_ _ _ _ _ _ _ _ _ _

```
200   YW = 4: YF$ = "."
210 PRINT "ENTER YOUR GUESS: ";
220 GOSUB 10000
230:
240 IF Z% = -1 THEN 4000: REM ESC TEST
260:
270   YW = 10: YF$ = "."
280 PRINT "ENTER A WORD: ";
290 GOSUB 10000
300 REM     PROGRAM CONTINUES
  :
  :
  :
3999 STOP
```

RUN the program now and "exercise" the data entry routine so that you can answer these questions.

1. What happens if you attempt to enter more characters than are acceptable?

2. What happens if you press the left arrow key?

3. What happens if you press CTRL C?

4. What happens if you press the ESC key?

— — — — — — — — — —

1.   The last character erases and is replaced by the most recent character typed. You cannot enter more characters than allowed.
2.   The previous character(s) is erased and can be replaced by a new character. This allows the user to correct data entry mistakes.
3.   Nothing. The CTRL key is deactivated.
4.   ESC flashes on the screen until you press some other key. If you attempt to enter data, ESC is erased and the data are accepted.

A Technical Peek at the General-Purpose Subroutine

This short subroutine is very powerful in terms of what it does. Line 10000 sets the field-filler character to the default condition blank if it has not already been set by the program. Lines 10010 and 10020 establish the cursor position for later use. The subroutine at 10500 prints the field-filler characters on the screen to establish the data entry screen.

The only actual point to enter data is the GET statement in line 10110. Note that the entry is to a string variable (Z1$) so that numbers, letters, and special characters are all acceptable.

RETURN is checked in line 10120. ESC is tested in line 10130. Thereafter, the program handles the left-arrow-erase routine (10200 through 10230), ignores all unwanted characters (10300), and checks the length of data entry (10330 through 10350),

What happens in line 10410?

—————————————

The exit string, Z$, is created, one character at a time being concatenated to Z$.

INPUT NUMBER SUBROUTINE

The General-Purpose Input Subroutine can accept any entered data: numbers, letters, and special characters. We have designed two special subroutines to enter numeric values; the Input Integer Subroutine and the Input Decimal Subroutine. Here are the beginning statements of the Input Number Subroutine. It is used by the Integer and Decimal Subroutines:

```
10592   REM   * INPUT NUMBER *
10593   REM   ENTRY: CONDITIONS FOR INPUT STRING SET
10594   REM   EXIT:   Z% -1 (ESC); 0 (INVALID); 1 (INTEGER); 2 (DECIMAL)
10595   REM           Z  VALUE (IF VALID)
10599   :
10600   GOSUB 10000: REM  GET STRING
10610   IF Z% =  - 1 OR  LEN (Z$) = 0 THEN  RETURN : REM  ESC OR
        RETURN ONLY (Z%=0)
10620 Z% = 1: REM  SET VALID FLAG
10630   FOR Z1 = 1 TO  LEN (Z$):Z1$ =  MID$ (Z$,Z1,1)
10640   IF Z1$ = "." AND Z% = 1 THEN Z% = 2: GOTO 10660: REM  TRAP FOR
        FIRST DECIMAL POINT
10650   IF (Z1$ < "0" OR Z1$ > "9") AND (Z1$ <  > "-" AND Z1 > 1) THEN
        Z% = 0: REM  INVALID IF NOT A DIGIT AND NOT A LEADING -
10660   NEXT
10670 Z =  VAL (Z$): REM  VALUE ONLY IF VALID FLAG (Z%=1 OR 2)
10680   RETURN
10991   :
```

How to Use the Input Integer Subroutine

At times you will want the user to enter a positive or negative integer that falls within a range; for example, between 1 and 100. To enter a negative integer, use the minus (–) sign. For this situation a special integer subroutine is presented here.

The entry point for this subroutine is line 11000. Here is the Input Integer Subroutine:

```
10991 :
10992  REM   ** INPUT INTEGER **
10993  REM   ENTRY: CONDITIONS FOR INPUT STRING SET
10994  REM           YL  MINIMUM INTEGER
10995  REM           YH  MAXIMUM
10996  REM   EXIT:   Z%  -1 (ESC); 0 (INVALID INTEGER); 1 (VALID
       INTEGER)
10997  REM           Z   VALUE (IF INTEGER VALID)
10999 :
11000  GOSUB 10600: REM  INPUT NUMBER
11010  IF Z% < 1 THEN  RETURN : REM  ESC OR INVALID
11020  IF Z% = 2 THEN Z% = 0: RETURN : REM  INVALID IF DECIMAL POINT
11030  IF Z < YL OR Z > YH THEN Z% = 0: REM  INVALID IF OUT OF RANGE
11040  RETURN
```

The entry variables contain the low and high range of the acceptable integer. You will still want to set YW and YF$ for field width and filler character. Your program might look like this segment that will set the entry variables to accept a three-character integer in the range of 250 through 750:

```
200 YW = 3: YF$ = "-"
210   YL = 250: YH = 750
220 PRINT "ENTER A 3 - DIGIT NUMBER: ";
230 GOSUB 11000
240:
```

The exit variables from this subroutine are different than before. Z% returns as −1 if ESC was pressed. If the number entered falls within the 250 through 750 range, Z% will be set to 1. If the entered item is out of range or contains invalid characters, Z% is set to 0. This means that you must include an error test and message to advise the user to enter a number within range. The variable Z will contain the entered and accepted number. Here's how your subroutine exit tests might look:

```
250 IF Z% = −1 THEN 5000: REM ESC TEST
260 IF Z% = 0 THEN PRINT:PRINT "PLEASE ENTER A
NUMBER BETWEEN "; YL; " AND ";YH: GOTO 200:
REM INVALID NUMBER TEST
270 IF Z = N THEN 4000: REM WINNER ROUTINE
280:
```

How to Use the Input Decimal Subroutine

To enter numbers with decimals, or non-integer numbers, use the
Input Decimal Subroutine shown below:

```
11091  :
11092   REM   ** INPUT DECIMAL **
11093   REM   ENTRY: CONDITIONS FOR INPUT STRING SET
11094   REM          YL   MINIMUM VALUE
11095   REM          YH   MAXIMUM
11096   REM   EXIT:  Z%  -1 (ESC); 0 (INVALID); 1 (INTEGER); 2
        (DECIMAL)
11097   REM          Z    VALUE (IF VALID)
11099  :
11100   GOSUB 10600: REM   INPUT NUMBER
11110   IF Z% < 1 THEN  RETURN : REM  ESC OR INVALID
11120   IF Z < YL OR Z > YH THEN Z% = 0: REM   INVALID IF OUT OF RANGE
11130   RETURN
11191  :
11192   REM   ** INPUT Y OR N **
11193   REM   ENTRY: CURSOR AND FILLER CHARACTER SET
11194   REM   EXIT:  Z%  -1 (ESC); 0 (NEITHER Y NOR N); 1 (Y), 2 (N)
11199  :
```

The entry point is line 11100. The entry variables are the same, YL
and YH for the minimum and maximum values; YW and YF$ for
field length and field filler. The exit value, Z%, has an added ele-
ment. It becomes 2 if the number entered contains a decimal point.
Otherwise, its use is the same as the integer subroutine.

Y/N SUBROUTINE

Another "special case" data entry situation occurs when a single
character is entered. The typical case is shown below:

```
DO YOU WANT INSTRUCTION (Y/N):
```

This is a special subroutine that you can use to accept only the
letters Y or N:

```
11191 :
11192  REM  ** INPUT Y OR N **
11193  REM  ENTRY: CURSOR AND FILLER CHARACTER SET
11194  REM  EXIT: Z%  -1 (ESC); 0 (NEITHER Y NOR N); 1 (Y), 2 (N)
11199 :
11200  Y$ = "YN": REM  USE INPUT SINGLE CHARACTER ROUTINE
11291 :
11292  REM  ** INPUT SINGLE CHARACTER AND MATCH WITH VALID STRING **
11293  REM  ENTRY: CURSOR AND FILLER CHARACTER SET
11294  REM         Y$ STRING OF MATCH CHARACTERS
11295  REM  EXIT: Z%  -1 (ESC); 0 (CHARACTER NOT IN STRING); J (J-TH
       CHARACTER IN MATCH STRING)
11299 :
11300  YW = 1: REM  SET FIELD WIDTH
11310  GOSUB 10000
11320  IF Z% =  - 1 OR  LEN (Z$) = 0 THEN  RETURN : REM  ESC OR
       RETURN ONLY (Z%=0)
11330  Z% = 0: REM  SET NOT MATCHED FLAG
11340  FOR Z1 = 1 TO  LEN (Y$)
11350  IF Z$ = MID$ (Y$,Z1,1) THEN Z% = Z1: REM  MATCH IN POSITION
       Z1
11360  NEXT
11370  RETURN
```

How to Use the Y/N Subroutine

To use this subroutine to accept only Y for yes or N for no, this is all
you must do:

```
200  YF$ = "-": REM  SET FILLER CHARACTER
210 GOSUB 11200
220 :
```

The exit variable Z% will be set to −1 if the user pressed ESC, to 0 if
neither Y or N was entered, to 1 if Y was entered, and to 2 if N was
entered. Your exit test statements might look like this:

```
230 IF Z% = −1 THEN 5000 : REM   ESC TEST
240 IF Z% = 0 THEN PRINT : PRINT "PLEASE ENTER Y OR N
ONLY": GOTO 200: REM INVALID ENTRY
250 IF Z% = 1 THEN GOSUB 8000 : REM   PRINT
INSTRUCTIONS IF Y
260 REM   CONTINUE PROGRAM
```

SINGLE-CHARACTER SUBROUTINE

Another subroutine included in the INPUT MODULE allows you to
enter any single character, not just Y or N. The entry point for this

subroutine is 11300. Before you enter the subroutine, you must set the filler character (YF$), and this time set Y$ to contain all acceptable characters. For example, if you want to accept any single character of A, E, I, O, or U, then set your variables like this:

```
250   YF$ = "-"
260   Y$ = "AEIOU"
270 PRINT "ENTER YOUR LETTER: ";
280 GOSUB 11300
```

The exit variable is still Z%, but the values mean different things. If Z% is −1, ESC has been pressed. If Z% is 0, the entered character is not valid. If Z% is a positive number, that number tells you which character number in Y$ was entered. For example, if the user entered the letter I, then Z% would be 3, indicating the third character in Y$ (AEIOU).

PAUSE OR KEYSTROKE SUBROUTINE

A common problem in games is how long to wait after the player has entered a guess before the program asks for another guess. If the program's response is "YOUR LETTER IS NOT IN MY WORD," "PLEASE GUESS A NUMBER BETWEEN 1 AND 40," or some other phrase, the player needs time to read and digest it before continuing. If the pause is too short, the novice player doesn't have enough time; too long, and the experienced player gets bored. The Pause or Keystroke Subroutine allows the programmer to pick a pause that will be long enough for the novice, but if the player types a keystroke the pause immediately ends (usually by asking for another guess) and the keystroke pressed will be accepted as part of the next input.

We recommend that you put this capability into your games and let the player discover it; we recommend against trying to explain it with additional instructions as it will tend to confuse the novice player and clutter the screen. This subroutine can be separated from the INPUT MODULE and used by itself in your programs.

```
11391 :
11392  REM  ** PAUSE OR UNTIL KEYSTROKE **
11393  REM  ENTRY: YP  LENGTH OF PAUSE IN INTERNAL TIME UNITS
11394  REM             0  WAIT FOR KEYSTROKE ONLY
11395  REM  EXIT:  Z%  -1 (ESC); 0 (PAUSE EXPIRED); 1 (KEYSTROKE
         BEFORE PAUSE EXPIRED)
11396  REM             Z  KEYSTROKE (ASCII VALUE + 128)
11399 :
11400  POKE  - 16368,0: REM  CLEAR TYPE-AHEAD
11410  Z1 = 0: REM  INITIALIZE COUNT (* ENTRY FOR GET ONE KEY *)
11420  Z1 = Z1 + 1
11430  Z =  PEEK ( - 16384)
11440  IF  Z >  = 128 THEN Z% = 1 - 2 * (Z = 155): RETURN : REM
         KEYSTROKE; TRAP FOR ESC THEN RETURN
11450  IF Z1 < YP OR YP = 0 THEN 11420
11460  Z% = 0: REM  PAUSE EXPIRED
```

The entry variable YP defaults to zero unless otherwise set. When YP is zero, the user must press a key to continue. Otherwise, the length of the pause is determined by an internal time unit. You should experiment with different time lengths.

The exit variable Z% sets to –1 if ESC was pressed, to 0 if the pause timed out, and to 1 if the user pressed a key before the time was up. You can use the latter two items of information or simply disregard them. Here are a sample entry and exit variable setting for this subroutine:

```
300 REM   INSTRUCTIONS HERE
310:
320 LET YP = 100
330 GOSUB 11400
340:
350 IF Z% = –1 THEN 5000; REM   ESC TEST
360 IF Z% = 0 THEN PRINT "IF YOU NEED MORE TIME,
CONTACT YOUR INSTRUCTOR":GOTO 300
370 REM   CONTINUE
```

GET ONE KEYSTROKE, NO ECHO SUBROUTINE

Another common problem in games is how long to wait after displaying instructions. The difference in reading speeds and familiarity with the game may require that the player signal the game to continue (by pressing a key), rather than the programmer trying to guess how long to wait.

Both the "Get One Key, No Echo, No Type-Ahead" at line 11500 and "Get One Key, No Echo, With Type-Ahead" at line 11600 wait until any one key is pressed (without also waiting for RETURN) and do not "echo" or display the key pressed on the screen. Unlike the Pause or Keystroke Subroutine, the key is "thrown away" and will not become part of the input. The exit variable Z% is set to −1 if ESC was the key, and to 1 if any other key was pressed. The variable Z is set to the ASCII value +128 of the key pressed. There are no entry variables.

The difference between these two subroutines involves "type-ahead." The APPLE hardware has a one-character "memory" that latches the last keystroke pressed. Reading the keyboard involves waiting for this latch to be set, then actually reading it, and finally clearing it to signal that a key has not just been pressed. (Refer to your *APPLE II Reference Manual* for more details if you wish.) The No Type-Ahead Subroutine at 11500 first clears the latch, then waits for a keystroke. Clearing the latch first forces the user to press a key AFTER the instructions (or whatever) have been displayed and the program logic is waiting for the next key. The With Type-Ahead Subroutine allows the experienced user to anticipate the pause and to avoid it; however, if the novice user inadvertently presses an extra key, the pause would also be skipped. We recommend using the No Type-Ahead version of this subroutine for this application.

For those of you who may be interested, a different version of these subroutines appears in the version of SIMON in Chapter 7. Notice line 3000, which gets the next note and THEN decides where to echo it.

The programs in Chapters 1 through 4 have not used the data entry testing techniques described in this chapter. If you plan to use any of those earlier programs, you should first merge them with INPUT MODULE and add necessary linkage statements to the programs.

DATA ENTRY SUBROUTINE REFERENCE SUMMARY

When using these subroutines, it is best to simply merge the entire INPUT MODULE with your program. If you use only the Pause or Keystroke Subroutine, delete the rest of INPUT MODULE and merge only that routine. The entire module does not take that much memory space for you to worry about chopping into pieces and merging only the pieces you need. Merge it all. It's much easier!

General-Purpose Subroutine

Entry point:	GOSUB 10000
Entry variables:	YW : field length
	YF$: field filler (default is blank)
Exit variables:	Z$: string entered
	Z% : 1 (ESC); 0 (not ESC)

Input Number Subroutine

This subroutine must also use the General-Purpose Subroutine.
   Integer Numbers

Entry point:	GOSUB 11000
Entry variables:	YW : field length
	YF$: field filler
	YL : minimum value
	YH : maximum value
Exit variables:	Z : value
	Z% : 1(ESC); 0 (invalid integer); 1 (valid integer)

   Decimal Numbers
ENTRY POINT: GOSUB 11100

Entry variables:	YW : field length
	YF$: field filler
	YL : minimum value
	YH : maximum value
Exit variables:	Z : value
	Z%: –1(ESC); 0 (invalid number); 1 (valid integer); 2 (decimal number)

Y/N Subroutine

This subroutine must also use the General-Purpose Subroutine.

Entry point: GOSUB 11200
Entry variables: YF$: field filler
Exit variables: Z% : −1 (ESC); 0 (neither Y nor N); 1 (Y); 2 (N)

General-Purpose Single-Character Subroutine

This subroutine must also use the General-Purpose Subroutine.

Entry point: GOSUB 11300
Entry variables: Y$: match characters
                    YF$: field filler
Exit variables: Z% : −1 (ESC); 0 (char. not in match string); J (Jth
                         position in match string)

Pause or Keystroke Subroutine

Entry point: GOSUB 11400
Entry variables: YP : LENGTH OF PAUSE
Exit variables: Z% : −1 (ESC); 0 (pause expired); 1 (keystroke
                         before pause expired)

Get One Key, No Echo, No Type-Ahead Subroutine

Entry point: GOSUB 11500
Entry variables: none
Exit variables: Z% : −1 (ESC), 1 (other way)
                    Z : ASCII value + 128 of keystroke

Get One Key, No Echo, with Type-Ahead Subroutine

Entry point :   GOSUB 11600
Entry variables: none
Exit variables :   Z% : −1 (ESC), 1 (other way)
                   Z : ASCII value + 128 of keystroke

CHAPTER SUMMARY

This chapter has given you the third complete program module that you can use when writing your own game programs. It is also an excellent subroutine to use when writing programs for any other purpose as well. The subroutine gives you complete control over what is acceptable data entry by the program user. We will show you how we use the data entry subroutine in our game programs that follow in the next chapters.

CHAPTER SIX

Text-Based Games

String variable manipulation, or doing things with text provided by the user, is the backbone of some of the "classic" and most interesting computer games. Although technical advances have provided us with color, graphics, and sound, word games continue to be fascinating, both to play and to write.

This chapter discusses word games that take advantage of the text manipulation capabilities of your APPLE and also suggests how to match the particular game to its intended audience. We will consider three types of word games—story construction, word guessing, and word matching. For each, we will build whole games and then discuss the reasons for the particular features included.

STORY

STORY asks a series of questions and inserts the answers in a previously constructed format. It uses a powerful game design that can be modified for any audience. You may recognize our version as a variation of the "mad-lib" games popular with school children.

```
10   REM   ...STORY-INPUT IMAGE...
11 :
997 :
998   REM   ** ONE-TIME INITIALIZATION **
999 :
1000   DIM RP$(10,10): REM   MAX # OF RANDOM GROUPS BY MAX # OF ITEMS
   IN EACH GROUP
1010   DIM NR(10): REM   ACTUAL # OF ITEMS IN EACH GROUP
1020   DIM A$(10): REM   MAX # OF ANSWERS
1197 :
1198   REM  * COVER SCREEN *
1199 :
1200   GR : HOME : COLOR= 15: GOSUB 15500: REM   WASH IN WHITE
1210   COLOR= 6: FOR Z = 11 TO 33 STEP 11: REM   BLUE LINES
1220   HLIN 0,39 AT Z - 8
1230   HLIN 0,39 AT Z
1240   NEXT
1250   X$ = "WRITE":XV = 4:XC(1) = 0: GOSUB 15300
1260   X$ = "A":XV = XV + 11: GOSUB 15300
1270   X$ = "STORY":XV = XV + 11: GOSUB 15300
1280   VTAB 23: HTAB 7: PRINT "PRESS RETURN TO CONTINUE...";
1290   GOSUB 11500: REM   WAIT FOR KEYSTROKE
1300   IF Z% = - 1 THEN  END : REM   ESC
1997 :
1998   REM   ** INITIALIZATION FOR NEXT STORY **
1999 :
2000   TEXT : HOME
2010   Z = 51000: GOSUB 19000: REM   SET READ DATA POINTER TO RANDOM
   PARTS
2097 :
2098   REM  * LOAD RANDOM STORY PARTS *
2099 :
2100   RP = 0
2110   J = 0
2120   READ Z$: REM  * SHARE LOGIC WITH NEW GROUP STARTED
2200   RP = RP + 1: REM   NEXT GROUP OF STORY PARTS
2210   J = 0: REM   # OF PARTS IN CURRENT GROUP
2230   IF Z$ = "END" THEN 2300
2240   J = J + 1
2250   RP$(RP,J) = Z$: REM   SAVE PART
2260   READ Z$
2270   GOTO 2230
2300   NR(RP) = J: REM   # OF RANDOM PARTS IN GROUP RP
2310   READ Z$: REM   CHECK FOR SECOND "END"
2320   IF Z$ = "END" THEN 2500: REM   NO MORE RANDOM PARTS
2330   GOTO 2200: REM   SHARE LOGIC TO BEGIN NEW GROUP
2497 :
2498   REM  * ASK QUESTIONS AND SAVE ANSWERS *
2499 :
2500   NQ = 0
2510   HTAB 14: PRINT "*** STORY ***"
2520   VTAB 22: HTAB 11: PRINT "PRESS ";: INVERSE : PRINT "ESC";:
   NORMAL ; PRINT " TO STOP.";
2600   READ Q$: REM   CHECK IF ANY MORE QUESTIONS
2610   IF Q$ = "END" THEN 3000: REM   NO MORE QUESTIONS
2620   NQ = NQ + 1: REM   ONE MORE QUESTION
2630   VTAB 2 * NQ + 4: HTAB 1: PRINT Q$;" ";
2640   YW = 38 - LEN (Q$): REM   MAXIMUM LENGTH OF ANSWER
2650   GOSUB 10000
2660   IF Z% = - 1 THEN 6000: REM   ESC
2670   IF  LEN (Z$) = 0 THEN 2650: REM   TRAP FOR EMPTY ANSWER
2680   A$(NQ) = Z$: REM   SAVE NEXT ANSWER
2690   GOTO 2600
2997 :
2998   REM   ** WRITE STORY **
2999 :
3000   HOME : REM   PAUSE BEFORE WRITING STORY
3010   SPEED= 10
3020   VTAB 11: HTAB 9
3030   PRINT "HERE IS YOUR STORY."; CHR$ (7);".."; CHR$ (7);".."; CHR$
   (7)
3040   SPEED= 255
3050   YP = 50: GOSUB 11400: REM   PAUSE OR UNTIL KEYSTROKE
```

```
3091 :
3092  REM  * WRITE STORY FROM STORY PARTS IN DATA STATEMENTS *
3093  REM  TRAP FOR WORDS BREAKING IN THE MIDDLE AT THE END OF A
      LINE
3099 :
3100 L = 3: REM  LEFT MARGIN (FOR TEXT WINDOW)
3110 W = 34: REM  WIDTH
3120 T = 4: REM  TOP LINE
3130 B = 20: REM  BOTTOM
3140  POKE 32,L: REM  SET TEXT WINDOW
3150  REM  WIDTH SETTING IS NOT NEEDED
3160  POKE 34,T
3170  POKE 35,B
3180  HOME : REM  MOVE CURSOR TO ULHC OF WINDOW
3200 S$ = "": REM  INITIALIZE SCREEN LINE
3210  READ Z$: REM  NEXT STORY ELEMENT
3220  IF Z$ = "END" THEN 3900: REM  END OF STORY
3230  IF LEFT$ (Z$,1) = "#" THEN 3500: REM  USE ANSWER NUMBER
      SPECIFIED
3240  IF LEFT$ (Z$,1) = "@" THEN 3600: REM  USE RANDOM PART FROM
      GROUP SPECIFIED
3300 S$ = S$ + Z$: REM  APPEND STORY PART
3310  IF LEN (S$) < = W THEN 3210: REM  SCREEN LINE NOT YET FULL
3320 Z = W + 1: REM  TRY TO BREAK THE LINE AT THE RIGHTMOST BLANK
      POSSIBLE
3330  REM  START WITH THE FIRST CHARACTER BEYOND THE MAXIMUM WIDTH
3340  IF Z = 1 THEN Z = W + 1: GOTO 3400: REM  NO BLANKS ANYWHERE;
      USE MAXIMUM WIDTH
3350  IF MID$ (S$,Z,1) = " " THEN 3400: REM  FOUND BLANK AT
      POSITION Z
3360 Z = Z - 1
3370  GOTO 3340
3400  PRINT LEFT$ (S$,Z - 1): REM  BREAK THE LINE AT THE Z-TH
      CHARACTER
3410  IF Z = LEN (S$) THEN 3200: REM  NOTHING LEFT OVER
3420 S$ = RIGHT$ (S$, LEN (S$) - Z): REM  REST OF THE LINE
3430  GOTO 3310: REM  CHECK IF STILL TOO LONG
3500 Z$ = A$( VAL ( RIGHT$ (Z$, LEN (Z$) - 1))): REM  USE ANSWER
      NUMBER SPECIFIED
3510  GOTO 3300
3600 Z = VAL ( RIGHT$ (Z$, LEN (Z$) - 1)): REM  RAMDOM GROUP
      SPECIFIED
3610 Z$ = RP$(Z,1 + INT (NR(Z) * RND (1))): REM  PICK ONE
3620  GOTO 3300
3900  IF LEN (S$) > 0 THEN PRINT S$: REM  * END OF STORY - PRINT
      REMAINING PART *
3910  TEXT : REM  SET FULL SCREEN WINDOW
5997 :
5998  REM  ** AGAIN? **
5999 :
6000  HTAB 1: VTAB 24
6010  PRINT "ANOTHER STORY (Y OR N)? ";
6020  GOSUB 11200: REM  Y/N
6030  ON Z% + 2 GOTO 6100,6000,2000,6100: REM  ESC, INVALID, Y, N
6100  PRINT : PRINT
6110  PRINT "THANKS FOR PLAYING.";
6120  END
50991 :
50992  REM  * RANDOM STORY PARTS, ENDING WITH "END" *
50993  REM  EACH GROUP ENDS WITH "END"
50994  REM  TO OMIT RANDOM GROUPS, '51000 DATA "END","END"'
50999 :
51000  DATA  "ON HALLOWEEN,", "ONE DARK NIGHT,", "END": REM  *
       RANDOM 1 *
51010  DATA  "RUNNING", "SITTING", "SKATING", "END": REM  * RANDOM
       2 *
51020  DATA  "AT THE SEASHORE", "IN THE MOUNTAINS", "IN A HAUNTED
       HOUSE", "TO SCHOOL", "IN THE DESERT", "END": REM  * RANDOM 3 *
51030  DATA  "HEARD", "NOTICED", "END": REM  * RANDOM 4 *
51040  DATA  "SLIMY", "HUGE", "FUZZY", "FURRY", "END": REM  * RANDOM
       5 *
51050  DATA  "KISSED", "PINCHED", "PLAYED CHESS WITH", "SKATED ALONG
       WITH", "READ STORIES TO", "END": REM  * RANDOM 6 *
```

```
51060  DATA  "BROUGHT THEM ALL SOME BIRTHDAY CAKE", "FLEW THEM AWAY
       IN A HELICOPTER", "SANG THEM A LULLABY", "END": REM  * RAMDOM 7 *
51070  DATA  "END": REM  END RANDOM GROUPS
51991  :
51992  REM  * QUESTIONS, ENDING WITH "END" *
51999  :
52000  DATA  "WHAT'S YOUR NAME?"
52010  DATA  "WHAT'S YOUR FAVORITE COLOR?"
52020  DATA  "WHOM DO YOU LOVE?"
52030  DATA  "WHAT ARE YOU AFRAID OF?"
52040  DATA  "WHO'S YOUR BEST FRIEND?"
52050  DATA  "END"
52991  :
52992  REM  * STORY, ENDING WITH "END"*
52993  REM  TYPES OF DATA:
52994  REM    "#NUMBER" = PRINT ANSWER NUMBER
52995  REM    "@NUMBER" = PRINT ONE FROM RANDOM GROUP NUMBER
52996  REM    "END"     = END OF STORY (DOESN'T PRINT)
52997  REM    ELSE      = PRINT AS TEXT STRING
52999  :
53000  DATA  "@1"," "
53010  DATA  "#1"," AND ","#5"
53020  DATA  " WERE ","@2"," ","@3",". ALL OF A SUDDEN THEY "
53030  DATA  "@4"," A ","@5"," "
53040  DATA  "#2"," ","#4"
53050  DATA  ". THE "
53060  DATA  "#2"," ","#4"
53070  DATA  " ALMOST ","@6"," THEM BUT ALONG CAME "
53080  DATA  "#3"
53090  DATA  " AND ","@7",". "
53100  DATA  "END"
60000  :
60010  REM  * COPYRIGHT 1981 BY HOWARD FRANKLIN, PALO ALTO, CA *
60020  :
```

Merge this with INPUT MODULE and IMAGE MODULE. SAVE it as STORY and RUN it.

This is the original STORY program, rewritten to include INPUT checking and screen formatting for the Apple. STORY was written at the Community Computer Center and first appeared in print in 1976 in an early People's Computer Company newspaper. Developed for use with teletypes, STORY was designed to be fun and also to be a good language exercise for beginning readers. Notice that the questions ask for very personal answers. Children remember these personal responses easily, so it is not difficult for them to "read" the story the computer displays. STORY differs from other mad-lib games by asking for answers to specific questions rather than for parts of speech.

Unlike more traditional games, STORY has no winner or loser. Hence, older children and even adults find it an enjoyable, non-threatening introduction to computers. In fact, STORY can easily be turned into an introduction to programming for more sophisticated players. After several runs of the program, players see a pattern in the story construction and begin to understand what the program is doing. You might want to explain how computer programs work, basing your explanation on their experience with STORY.

Notice that the questions are constructed so that the players can answer either with one word or a longer phrase. If the answers match the questions grammatically, they will fit properly into the following story structure. However, the length of the answer is limited. Examine line 2640.

1.   What would happen if you changed a question so it became thirty-five characters long?

2.   How would you change the program to ask different questions?

—— —— —— —— —— —— —— ——

1.   The answer would be limited to three characters.
2.   Change the data statements in lines 52000 through 52050.

Breaking words arbitrarily at the end of a line and continuing the word on the next line is called wraparound. Wraparound can be unpleasant, yet many text-based programs suffer from it. A routine included in STORY avoids wrapping words around the screen. The routine checks for spaces (ends of words) and breaks the line at a suitable spot. You may want to use this routine in other programs you write.

What part of the program handles the problem of screen wraparound?

—— —— —— —— —— —— —— ——

Lines 3310 through 3430

Consider changing STORY to suit your particular audience. Be sure to match the wording, content, and length of the story to the reading ability and/or sophistication level of your intended audience.

Here's how to change the text part of the story. Look at lines 50000 through 51070. They contain the randomly selected phrases for the story. Each series of phrases ends with the word "END" followed by a REM. (The "END" is required; the REM is, of course, optional.)

```
51000 DATA "ON HALLOWEEN,",", "ONE DARK
NIGHT,",", "END":REM *RANDOM1*
```

Line 51000 indicates that only two choices are possible for random phrase 1.

Our program has seven sets of phrases.

How many phrase choices are there for phrase 3?

— — — — — — — —

Line 51020. Four choices.

You can change the text of the story by changing these phrase choices. Be careful to use the same format used in the program.

Changing the format of the story is a little more difficult. The code for the story is as follows:

```
52992  REM  * STORY, ENDING WITH "END"*
52993  REM  TYPES OF DATA:
52994  REM    "#NUMBER" = PRINT ANSWER NUMBER
52995  REM    "@NUMBER" = PRINT ONE FROM RANDOM GROUP NUMBER
52996  REM    "END"     = END OF STORY (DOESN'T PRINT)
52997  REM    ELSE      = PRINT AS TEXT STRING
52999  :
53000  DATA  "@1"," "
53010  DATA  "#1"," AND ","#5"
53020  DATA  " WERE ","@2"," ","@3",". ALL OF A SUDDEN THEY "
53030  DATA  "@4"," A ","@5"," "
53040  DATA  "#2"," ","#4"
53050  DATA  ". THE "
53060  DATA  "#2"," ","#4"
53070  DATA  " ALMOST ","@6"," THEM BUT ALONG CAME "
53080  DATA  "#3"
53090  DATA  " AND ","@7","."
53100  DATA  "END"
```

Lines 52994 through 52997 tell you how to make the story, followed by the format of the current story that you played. To cause the user-entered answer to display on the screen, use the @ symbol, followed by the question answer number, as shown in line 53080.

The user's third response will be printed in response to the DATA in line 53080.

To select one of the random phrases, use the @ symbol, followed by the group number of the phrases. Line 53000 above will cause the selection of one of the random phrases labeled "random 1" in line 51000. Anything else in your story will print as you type it. Notice the words in lines 53020 and 53070. You end the story by typing "END," as shown in line 53100.

You will find that matching story phrases to question responses takes practice and experience. The more you do, the better your stories will be. Your friends of all ages will enjoy your stories.

BLOCKOUT

BLOCKOUT has its origins in a game called Hangman. An earlier version, called SNAKE, was designed at the Community Computer Center and published in *People's Computer Company* newspaper, along with STORY. SNAKE, written for teletype printers, was originally intended to incorporate Hangman's educational potential, yet eliminate the waste of paper caused by redrawing the gallows, the inherent gruesomeness of the game, and the relatively fixed number of tries until failure.

BLOCKOUT preserves the spirit of SNAKE while making use of the graphic capabilities of your APPLE.

```
10   REM   ...BLOCKOUT-INPUT SOUND IMAGE...
11 :
997 :
998   REM   ** ONE-TIME INITIALIZATION **
999 :
1000  DIM WD$(50)
1010 ML = 16: REM  MAXIMUM LENGTH OF SECRET WORD
1020 HG = 8: REM  HORIZONTAL TAB FOR GUESS
1030 HC = HG + ML + 1: REM  HORIZONTAL TAB FOR CLUE
1040 VG = 21: REM  VERTICAL TAB FOR GUESS
1050 VC = VG: REM  VERTICAL TAB FOR CLUE
1100 NW = 0: REM  * COUNT THE WORDS AND STORE THEM IN WD$(J) *
1110 Z = 51000: GOSUB 19000: REM  READ DATA FROM LINE 51000
1120  READ Z$
1130  IF Z$ = "END" THEN 1200: REM  NO MORE WORDS
1140  IF  LEN (Z$) > ML THEN 1120: REM  THROW AWAY WORD IF TOO LONG
1150 NW = NW + 1: REM  ONE MORE WORD
1160 WD$(NW) = Z$
1170  GOTO 1120
1200 NG = 10: REM  DEFAULT # OF INCORRECT GUESSES
1210 GU = 15: REM  UPPER BOUND ON # OF GUESSES
1220 GL = 5: REM  LOWER BOUND
1300  DIM BK%(15,1): REM  H/V POSITIONS OF THE BLOCKS
1310 BH = 2: REM  HORIZONTAL WIDTH
1320 BV = 3: REM  VERTICAL HEIGHT
1397 :
1398  REM  * COVER SCREEN *
1399 :
1400  GR : HOME : COLOR= 1: GOSUB 15500: REM  WASH IN RED
1410  COLOR= 0: FOR J = 1 TO 80: REM  RANDOM BLOCKS IN BLACK
1420 XH =  INT (37 *  RND (1)) + 1:XV =  INT (36 *  RND (1)) + 1: REM
     RANDOM ULHC
1430  FOR Z = 0 TO 2: HLIN XH,XH + 1 AT XV + Z: NEXT
1440  NEXT
1450 XC(1) = 15:XV = 12:X$ = "BLOCK": GOSUB 15300
1460 XV = XV + XB + 2:X$ = "OUT": GOSUB 15300
1470 .VTAB 23: HTAB 6: PRINT "PRESS RETURN TO CONTINUE...";
1480  GOSUB 11500: REM  WAIT FOR KEYSTROKE
1490  IF Z% =  - 1 THEN  END : REM  ESC
1900  GOSUB 9000: REM  INSTRUCTIONS
1997 :
1998  REM  ** INITIALIZATION FOR NEXT GAME **
1999 :  .
2000  IF NW = 0 THEN 6800: REM  NO MORE WORDS
2010 Z =  INT (NW *  RND (1)) + 1
2020 SW$ = WD$(Z): REM  PICK ONE OF THE UNUSED WORDS
2030 WD$(Z) = WD$(NW): REM  REPLACE THE CHOSEN "SLOT" WITH THE LAST
     UNUSED WORD
2040 NW = NW - 1: REM  AND REDUCE THE SIZE OF THE UNUSED WORD LIST
     BY 1
2100 L$ = "": REM  INITIALIZE L$,U$,C$, AND BL$
2110 U$ = ""
2120 C$ = ""
2130  FOR J = 1 TO 26
2140 L$ = L$ +  CHR$ (64 + J): REM  NEXT LETTER OF THE ALPHABET
2150 U$ = U$ + " ": REM  ONE MORE BLANK
2160 C$ = C$ + "-": REM  ONE MORE -
2170  NEXT
2180 C$ =  LEFT$ (C$, LEN (SW$)): REM  SHORTEN CLUES TO LENGTH OF
     SECRET WORD
2190 BL$ = U$ + U$: REM  52 BLANKS
2300  GOSUB 9500: REM  SETUP
2997 :
2998  REM  ** NEXT GUESS **
2999 :
3000  VTAB VG: HTAB HG
3010 YW = 1: GOSUB 10000
3020  IF Z% =  - 1 THEN 6200: REM  ESC
3030  IF Z$ < "A" OR Z$ > "Z" THEN 4700: REM  NOT A LETTER OF THE
     ALPHABET
3100  REM  CHECK IF LETTER HAS ALREADY BEEN GUESSED
3110 Z =  ASC (Z$) -  ASC ("A") + 1: REM  POSITION IN U$
3120  IF  MID$ (U$,Z,1) <  > " " THEN 4600: REM  ALREADY USED
```

```
3130  REM  UPDATE L$ AND U$ AND DISPLAY
3140  REM  SPECIAL CASE FOR STRING FUNCTIONS IF FIRST OR LAST
      CHARACTER
3150  IF Z = 1 THEN L$ = " " +  RIGHT$ (L$,25):U$ = Z$ +  RIGHT$
      (U$,25)
3160  IF Z = 26 THEN L$ =  LEFT$ (L$,25) + " ":U$ =  LEFT$ (U$,25) +
      Z$
3170  IF Z > 1 AND Z < 26 THEN L$ =  LEFT$ (L$,Z - 1) + " " +  RIGHT$
      (L$,26 - Z):U$
      =  LEFT$ (U$,Z - 1) + Z$ +  RIGHT$ (U$,26 - Z)
3180  VTAB 23: HTAB HG: PRINT U$
3190  HTAB HG: PRINT L$;
3397  :
3398  REM  CHECK IF LETTER IS IN THE WORD
3399  :
3400  REM  SUBSTITUTE ALL OCCURRENCES IN C$ (CLUE) OF THE GUESS, IF
      ANY
3410  REM  DUE TO LIMITATIONS OF THE STRING FUNCTIONS, C$ IS REBUILT
      ONE LETTER AT A TIME
3420  Z1$ = ""
3430  FOR J = 1 TO  LEN (SW$)
3440  Z2$ =  MID$ (SW$,J,1): REM  NEXT SECRET LETTER
3450  IF Z$ = Z2$ THEN Z1$ = Z1$ + Z$: REM  GUESS MATCHES A SECRET
      LETTER
3460  IF Z$ <  > Z2$ THEN Z1$ = Z1$ +  MID$ (C$,J,1): REM  NO MATCH,
      USE INFORMATION FROM CLUE
3470  NEXT
3480  IF Z1$ = C$ THEN 4000: REM  CLUE HAS NOT CHANGED SO GUESS IS
      INCORRECT
3490  C$ = Z1$: REM  A CORRECT GUESS; UPDATE CLUE AND DISPLAY (ENTRY
      FOR CORRECT WORD GUESSED)
3500  VTAB VC: HTAB HC: PRINT C$;
3510  GOTO 5000
3997  :
3998  REM  ** INCORRECT GUESS **
3999  :
4000  J = NB
4010  FOR K = 1 TO 8: REM  FLASH LAST BLOCK
4020  J = NB
4030  GOSUB 8300
4040  YP = 2: GOSUB 11400: REM  PAUSE
4050  J = NB
4060  GOSUB 8400: REM  ERASE LAST BLOCK
4070  NEXT
4100  NB = NB - 1: REM  ONE LESS BLOCK
4110  IF NB > 0 THEN 3000: REM  BLOCKS STILL LEFT
4120  GOTO 6200
4597  :
4598  REM  * ERRORS *
4599  :
4600  Z$ = "THAT LETTER HAS ALREADY BEEN TRIED": REM  ALREADY GUESSED
4610  GOTO 4900
4700  Z$ = "PLEASE GUESS A LETTER FROM A TO Z": REM  NOT ALPHABETIC
4891  :
4892  REM  * DISPLAY ERROR MESSAGE AND PAUSE *
4893  REM  ENTRY: Z$  MESSAGE TO DISPLAY
4899  :
4900  VTAB 22: HTAB 20 -  LEN (Z$) / 2: REM  CENTER
4910  INVERSE : PRINT Z$;: NORMAL
4920  YP = 60: GOSUB 11400: REM  PAUSE
4930  HTAB 1: PRINT  LEFT$ (BL$,40): REM  CLEAR ERROR LINE
4940  GOTO 3000: REM  NEXT GUESS
4997  :
4998  REM  ** CORRECT GUESS **
4999  :
5000  IF C$ = SW$ THEN 5100: REM  ** CORRECT GUESS **
5010  REM  CORRECT LETTER BUT WORD NOT YET GUESSED
5020  W1 = 0:W2 = 1:W3 = 0:W4 = 10:W5 =  - 1:W6 = 50:W7 = 2: GOSUB
      13400
5030  FOR K = 1 TO 15
5040  J =  INT (NB *  RND (1)) + 1: REM  PICK A RANDOM BLOCK
5050  GOSUB 8300: REM  AND CHANGE ITS COLOR
5060  NEXT
5070  GOTO 3000: REM  NEXT GUESS
```

```
5100 WD = 100:Z$ = SW$: GOSUB 13300: REM  * GOT THE SECRET WORD *
5110  FOR K = 1 TO 4
5120  FOR J = 1 TO NB: GOSUB 8400: NEXT
5130  FOR J = 1 TO NB: GOSUB 8300: NEXT
5140  NEXT
5150  GOTO 6000: REM  AGAIN?
5997 :
5998  REM  ** AGAIN? **
5999 :
6000  POKE 34,22: HOME : REM  CLEAR BOTTOM 2 LINES
6010  VTAB 24: HTAB 1
6020  PRINT "PLAY AGAIN (Y OR N)? ";
6030  YF$ = " ": GOSUB 11200: REM  Y/N
6040  ON Z% + 2 GOTO 6100,6000,2000,6100: REM  ESC, INVALID, Y, N
6100  PRINT : PRINT
6110  PRINT "THANKS FOR PLAYING.";
6120  END
6197 :
6198  REM  * QUIT *
6199 :
6200  VTAB 22: HTAB HC - 14
6210  INVERSE : PRINT "THE WORD WAS: ";SW$: NORMAL
6220  GOTO 6000
6797 :
6798  REM  * NO MORE WORDS *
6799 :
6800  HOME
6810  PRINT
6820  PRINT "YOU HAVE USED ALL THE SECRET WORDS"
6830  GOTO 6100
7997 :
7998  REM  ** BLOCK ROUTINES **
7999 :
8000  POKE 34,20: HOME : REM  ** SET UP BLOCKS ** (CLEAR TEXT LINES)
8010  COLOR= 0: FOR Z = BT TO 39: HLIN 0,39 AT Z: NEXT : REM  CLEAR
      BLOCK AREA
8020  FOR J = 1 TO NB
8030  GOSUB 8100: REM  LOCATE AND DISPLAY NEXT BLOCK
8040  NEXT
8050  RETURN
8100  H =  INT ((40 - BH) *  RND (1)): REM  * LOCATE AND DISPLAY A
      BLOCK BELOW TITLE *
8110  REM  J = BLOCK #
8120  REM  DO NOT ALLOW BLOCK TO BE "TOO CLOSE" TO BLOCKS 1,...,J-1
8130  V =  INT ((39 - BV - BT) *  RND (1)) + BT
8140  IF J = 1 THEN 8210: REM  FIRST BLOCK LOCATED
8150  FOR Z = 1 TO J - 1
8160  IF  ABS (BK%(Z,0) - H) > BH OR  ABS (BK%(Z,1) - V) > BV THEN
      8200: REM  NOT TO 0 CLOSE
8170  H =  INT ((40 - BH) *  RND (1)): REM  PICK A NEW LOCATION
8180  V =  INT ((39 - BV - BT) *  RND (1)) + BT
8190  Z = 0: REM  AND BEGIN "CLOSENESS" CHECK AGAIN
8200  NEXT
8210  BK%(J,0) = H: REM  H-POS OF BLOCK J
8220  BK%(J,1) = V: REM  V-POS
8230  REM  FALL THROUGH TO DISPLAY A BLOCK
8300  C =  INT (15 *  RND (1)) + 1: REM  * DISPLAY A BLOCK *
8310  REM  J= BLOCK #
8320  COLOR= C: REM  SOLID BLOCK (ENTRY FOR ERASE BLOCK)
8330  H = BK%(J,0): REM  H-POS
8340  V = BK%(J,1): REM  V-POS
8350  IF  SCRN( H,V) = C THEN 8300: REM  PICK ANOTHER COLOR IF SAME
      AS BEFORE
8360  FOR Z = 1 TO BH
8370  VLIN V,V + BV - 1 AT H + Z - 1
8380  NEXT
8390  RETURN
8400  C = 0: REM   * ERASE A BLOCK *
8410  REM  J = BLOCK #
8420  GOTO 8320: REM  SHARE CODE
8500  J =  INT (NB *  RND (1)) + 1: REM  * MOVE A BLOCK *
8510  REM  ERASE A RANDOM BLOCK, OVERWRITE THE BLOCK WITH THE "LAST"
      BLOCK,
```

```
8520   REM   THEN LOCATE AND DISPLAY A NEW "LAST" BLOCK
8530   GOSUB 8400: REM   ERASE THE CHOSEN BLOCK
8540   BK%(J,0) = BK%(NB,0): REM   OVERWRITE BLOCK J WITH THE LAST BLOCK
8550   BK%(J,1) = BK%(NB,1)
8560   J = NB
8570   GOTO 8100: REM   LOCATE AND DISPLAY A NEW LAST BLOCK
8997   :
8998   REM   ** INSTRUCTIONS **
8999   :
9000   TEXT : HOME
9010   PRINT "BLOCKOUT IS A WORD GUESSING GAME."
9020   PRINT
9030   PRINT
9040   PRINT "THE COMPUTER PICKS A SECRET WORD AND"
9050   PRINT "DISPLAYS A DASH FOR EACH LETTER."
9060   PRINT "(A 6-LETTER SECRET WORD GETS 6 DASHES.)"
9070   PRINT
9080   PRINT "TRY TO GUESS THE LETTERS."
9090   PRINT
9100   PRINT "EACH CORRECT GUESS IS SHOWN IN THE"
9110   PRINT "SECRET WORD.   EACH INCORRECT GUESS"
9120   PRINT "MAKES ONE OF THE BLOCKS DISAPPEAR."
9130   PRINT
9140   PRINT "YOU BEGIN WITH ";NG;" BLOCKS.  TRY TO GUESS"
9150   PRINT "THE SECRET WORD BEFORE THEY DISAPPEAR."
9160   PRINT
9170   PRINT "PRESS ";: INVERSE : PRINT "ESC";: NORMAL : PRINT " TO
       QUIT."
9180   PRINT
9190   PRINT "PRESS RETURN TO CONTINUE... ";
9200   GOSUB 11500: REM   WAIT FOR KEYSTROKE
9210   IF Z% = - 1 THEN 6100: REM   ESC
9300   GR : HOME : REM   TITLE
9310   X$ = "BLOCK":XC(1) =  INT (15 *  RND (1)) + 1:XV = 0: GOSUB
       15300: REM   TITLE
9320   X$ = "OUT":XV = XV + XB + 1: GOSUB 15300
9330   BT = XV + XB + 1: REM   TOP OF BLOCK AREA
9340   RETURN
9497   :
9498   REM   ** SETUP **
9499   :
9500   NB = NG: REM   # OF BLOCKS
9510   GOSUB 8000: REM   SET UP BLOCKS
9520   VTAB VG: HTAB HG - 7: PRINT "GUESS:";
9530   VTAB VC: HTAB HC: PRINT C$
9540   PRINT
9550   PRINT "USED:   ";U$
9560   PRINT "LEFT:   ";L$;
9570   RETURN
50997  :
50998  REM   ** WORDS, ENDING WITH "END" **
50999  :
51000  DATA   "STRATEGY","MONOLITH","EXASPERATE","ASP"
51010  DATA   "TABLOID","LICHEN","TENT","ASTOUND"
51020  DATA   "VARY","QUIZ","SYCOPHANT","INLET"
51030  DATA   "SYLPH","INFINITE","GOAL","PIANISSIMO"
51040  DATA   "OXYGEN","WILT","TRUISM","CEREBRAL"
51050  DATA   "BRAVERY","BARB","AUGER"
51090  DATA   "END"
60000  :
60010  REM * COPYRIGHT 1981 BY HOWARD FRANKLIN, PALO ALTO, CA *
60020  :
```

Merge this with INPUT MODULE, SOUND MODULE (delete lines 18000 through 19999), and IMAGE MODULE. SAVE it as BLOCK-OUT. RUN it.

BLOCKOUT makes effective use of low-resolution color and movement. The words are drawn from a word list written in DATA statements in lines 51000 through 51090. You can change or add to the list of word choices. You have a maximum of fifty word choices (see line 1000.) Be sure to leave line 51090 as a "flag" to the computer that there are no more words. Currently, the game permits ten wrong tries.

How would you change the program to make the wrong-try limit six?

––––––––––––

1200 NG = 6

Notice that BLOCKOUT uses the ESC convention introduced in the previous chapter. To end the game and see the mystery word, players press ESC and then RETURN.

The colored blocks are placed at random on the screen, and colors are assigned to them at random.

How would you change the program to make the blocks all orange?

––––––––––––

8300 COLOR = 9, and delete line 8350

Look at the routine that begins at line 8100. This routine carefully checks to be sure that blocks are not placed too closely to one another, a truly elegant addition to the program that helps create a pleasant-to-look-at screen image.

Currently, the wrong answer makes one of the blocks flash colors and then disappear.

Where and how does the program make the block disappear?

— — — — — — — — — —

In lines 8400 through 8420. Then in lines 8300 through 8390 the block is colored black.

In many graphics games, the four-line text window at the bottom of the screen is not used to full advantage. Questions tend to scroll off the screen, leaving no information for the player who forgot what to do. In BLOCKOUT, the clues (letters used and letters remaining) stay on the screen. Only the question is refreshed. This is one way the four-line text window can be used effectively. In general, you should try to design the screen so that relevant clues remain visible throughout the game.

Did you notice as you played BLOCKOUT that only correct answers received the positive sound response? Incorrect answers changed the screen, but did not receive a positive sound. Reinforcing positive responses and ignoring, when possible, negative responses is a good technique to use when writing educational games.

Look carefully at the cover screen routine that begins at line 1400. You might think that all the activity on the screen requires a lot of program code. However, because IMAGE MODULE is so well-designed, we needed to do little actual programming to create a very attractive screen. When you look at the other programs in this book, notice how little programming code was needed to create the attractive cover screens.

MATCH

MATCH is a solitaire game that can also be played by several people taking turns. The object of the game is to match all the word pairs. Players can exit from the game at any time by pressing ESC and then pressing the RETURN key. When designing MATCH, we chose not to display the correct answers when the player chooses to end the game. By the process of elimination, a player can always "win" MATCH, so there is no need to give the answers. One of the nice things about the ESC convention in INPUT MODULE is that the programmer retains complete control over the effect of pressing ESC.

```
10   REM   ...MATCH-INPUT SOUND IMAGE...
11 :
997 :
998   REM   ** ONE-TIME INITIALIZATION **
999 :
1000   DIM L$(50),R$(50),L%(50),R%(30)
1010   BL$ = ""
1020   FOR J = 1 TO 40
1030   BL$ = BL$ + " "
1040   NEXT
1100   Z = 51000: GOSUB 19000: REM   SET READ DATA POINTER
1110   READ HL,HR,C$
1120   Z = HR - HL - LEN (C$): IF Z < 2 THEN   HOME : PRINT "CONNECTING
       WORD DOES NOT FIT": END
1130   IF Z / 2 < > INT (Z / 2) THEN HR = HR - 1: REM   FORCE SAME #
       OF SPACES ON BOTH SIDES OF CONNECTING WORD
1140   HC =   INT ((HL + HR) / 2)
1150   VO = 2
1160   VS = 2
1200   NP = 0: REM   INITIALIZE WORD PAIRS
1210   READ Z$,Z1$
1220   IF Z$ = "END" OR Z1$ = "END" THEN 1300: REM   NO MORE PAIRS
1230   NP = NP + 1: REM   ONE MORE PAIR
1240   L$(NP) = Z$
1250   R$(NP) = Z1$
1260   GOTO 1210
1300   NR = 8: REM   8 ROWS
1397 :
1398   REM   * COVER SCREEN *
1399 :
1400   GR : HOME : COLOR= 13: GOSUB 15500: REM   WASH IN YELLOW
1410   X$ = "MATCH":XV = 10: XC(1) = 2: GOSUB 15300
1420   X$ = "W" + CHR$ (1) +   CHR$ (2) + "CH":XV = 40 - XV - XB:XC(1)
       = 7: GOSUB 15300: REM   MIRROR IMAGE
1430   VTAB 23: HTAB 8: PRINT "PRESS RETURN TO CONTINUE...";
1440   GOSUB 11500: REM   WAIT FOR KEYSTROKE
1450   IF Z% = - 1 THEN   END : REM   ESC
1900   GOSUB 9000: REM   INSTRUCTIONS
1997 :
1998   REM   ** INITIALIZATION FOR NEXT GAME **
1999 :
2000   FOR J = 1 TO NP
2010   L%(J) = - J: REM   SET FLAG FOR INITIALIZING DISPLAY
2020   NEXT
2030   N = NP: REM   SCRAMBLE ALL THE PAIRS
2040   GOSUB 2900
2050   N = NR: REM   USE THE FIRST NR
2060   FOR J = 1 TO N
2070   R%(J) = L%(J): REM   COPY TO R%(1,...,NR)
2080   NEXT
2090   GOSUB 2900: REM   SCRAMBLE THE SAME PAIRS FOR THE LEFT SIDE
2200   GOSUB 9500: REM   INITIALIZE THE DISPLAY
2210   GOTO 3000
2900   FOR Z = N TO 2 STEP   - 1: REM   SCRAMBLE L%(1,...,N)
2910   Z% = Z * RND (1) + 1
2920   Z1 = L%(Z)
2930   L%(Z) = L%(Z%)
2940   L%(Z%) = Z1
2950   NEXT
2960   RETURN
```

```
2997 :
2998  REM  ** CHOOSE NEXT PAIR **
2999 :
3000  FOR Z = 1 TO N
3010  VTAB VO + VS * (NR - N + Z): REM  BUILD # MENU
3020  HTAB HC: PRINT Z;
3030  NEXT
3100  QP$ = "PICK A NUMBER OF A WORD ON THE LEFT: "
3110  GOSUB 3500
3120  P1 = J
3130  INVERSE : REM  DISPLAY LEFT STRING IN INVERSE
3140  GOSUB 8600
3150  NORMAL
3200  QP$ = "NOW PICK A NUMBER FROM THE RIGHT: "
3210  GOSUB 3500
3220  P2 = J
3230  INVERSE : REM  DISPLAY THE RIGHT STRING IN INVERSE
3240  GOSUB 8800
3250  NORMAL
3300  FOR Z = 1 TO N: REM  CLEAR # MENU
3310  VTAB VO + VS * (NR - N + Z): REM  V-POS
3320  HTAB HC: REM  H-POS
3330  PRINT " ";
3340  NEXT
3400  IF L%(P1) ( ) R%(P2) THEN 4000: REM  PAIR DOESN'T MATCH
3410  GOTO 5000: REM  A MATCH
3491 :
3492  REM  * COMMON CODE TO PICK A STRING *
3493  REM  ENTRY: QP$ PROMPT
3494  REM  EXIT:  J   CHOICE
3499 :
3500  VTAB 22: HTAB 1: PRINT QP$;
3510  YL = 1:YH = N:YW = 1: GOSUB 11000
3520  IF Z% = - 1 THEN 6100
3530  IF Z% = 0 THEN 3800: REM  INVALID
3540  J = Z
3550  HTAB 1: PRINT  LEFT$ (BL$,39);
3560  RETURN
3800  Q$ = "PLEASE PICK A NUMBER FROM 1 TO " + STR$ (N)
3810  P = 80
3820  GOSUB 3900
3830  GOTO 3500: REM  TRY AGAIN
3891 :
3892  REM  * DISPLAY MESSAGE LINE *
3893  REM  ENTRY: Q$ STRING TO DISPLAY
3894  REM        P  PAUSE
3899 :
3900  VTAB 24: HTAB 20 - INT ( LEN (Q$) / 2)
3910  INVERSE : PRINT Q$;: NORMAL
3920  YP = P: GOSUB 11400: REM  PAUSE
3930  HTAB 1: PRINT  LEFT$ (BL$,39);
3940  RETURN
3997 :
3998  REM  ** PAIR DOESN'T MATCH **
3999 :
4000  YP = 10
4010  IF P1 = P2 THEN 4400: REM  LEFT,RIGHT LINED UP
4020  IF P2 ( P1 THEN 4200: REM  MOVE RIGHT SIDE DOWN FIRST
4030  UD = 1: REM  MOVE LEFT SIDE DOWN ONE
4040  GOSUB 8000
4050  GOTO 4010
4200  UD = 1: REM  MOVE RIGHT SIDE DOWN ONE
4210  GOSUB 8200
4220  GOTO 4010
4400  IF P1 = N THEN 4600: REM  LEFT,RIGHT LINED UP AT THE BOTTOM
4410  UD = 1: REM  MOVE BOTH SIDES
4420  GOSUB 8400
4430  GOTO 4400
4600  W1 = 0:W2 = 5:W3 = 0:W4 = 10:W5 = 1:W7 = 1: GOSUB 13400
4610  Q$ = "** NOT A MATCH **"
4620  P = 60
4630  GOSUB 3900
4640  J = P1
4650  GOSUB 8600: REM  DISPLAY IN NORMAL
```

```
4660   GOSUB 8800
4670   GOTO 3000
4997 :
4998   REM  ** PAIR MATCHES **
4999 :
5000 YP = 10
5010   IF P1 = P2 THEN 5400: REM  LEFT,RIGHT LINED UP
5020   IF P2 > P1 THEN 5200: REM  MOVE RIGHT SIDE UP FIRST
5030 UD =  - 1: REM  MOVE LEFT SIDE UP ONE
5040   GOSUB 8000
5050   GOTO 5010
5200 UD =  - 1: REM  MOVE RIGHT SIDE UP ONE
5210   GOSUB 8200
5220   GOTO 5010
5400   IF P1 = 1 THEN 5600: REM  LEFT,RIGHT LINED UP AT THE TOP
5410 UD =  - 1: REM  MOVE BOTH SIDES
5420   GOSUB 8400
5430   GOTO 5400
5600 W1 = 0:W2 = 5:W3 = 0:W4 = 10:W5 =  - 1:W7 = 1: GOSUB 13400
5610   VTAB V0 + VS * (NR - N + 1): REM  LEFT,RIGHT ON TOP LINE
5620   HTAB HC -  INT ( LEN (C$) / 2)
5630   INVERSE : PRINT C$;: NORMAL
5640 Z$ = L$(L%(1))
5650 Z1$ = R$(R%(1))
5700   FOR J = HL + 1 TO HC -  INT ( LEN (C$) / 2) - 1: REM  MOVE THE
       WORDS TOGETHER
5710   HTAB J -  LEN (Z$) - 1: PRINT " ";: INVERSE : PRINT Z$;: NORMAL
5720   HTAB HR + HL - J: INVERSE : PRINT Z1$;: NORMAL : PRINT " ";
5730   NEXT
5800 Q$ = "YOU FOUND A MATCH!"
5810 P = 60
5820   GOSUB 3900
5830 N = N - 1: REM  ONE LESS PAIR
5840   IF N = 0 THEN 5900: REM  FOUND THEM ALL
5850   FOR J = 1 TO N: REM  MOVE THE LIST DOWN ONE
5860 L%(J) = L%(J + 1)
5870 R%(J) = R%(J + 1)
5880   NEXT
5890   GOTO 3000
5900   VTAB 21: HTAB 7: PRINT "YOU FOUND ALL THE MATCHES!!"
5997 :
5998   REM  ** AGAIN? **
5999 :
6000   HTAB 1: VTAB 24
6010   PRINT "PLAY AGAIN (Y OR N)? ";
6020   GOSUB 11200: REM  Y/N
6030   ON Z% + 2 GOTO 6100,6000,2000,6100: REM  ESC, INVALID, Y, N
6100   PRINT : PRINT
6110   PRINT "THANKS FOR PLAYING.";
6120   END
7997 :
7998   REM  ** MOVE ROUTINES **
7999 :
8000 Z = L%(P1): REM  MOVE LEFT SIDE DOWN/UP ONE
8010   REM  UD = -1 UP, +1 DOWN
8020 L%(P1) = L%(P1 + UD)
8030 L%(P1 + UD) = Z
8100 J = P1: REM  DISPLAY NEW LEFT J
8110   GOSUB 8700: REM  BLANK
8120   GOSUB 8600: REM  THEN DISPLAY
8130 J = P1 + UD:P1 = J: REM  MOVE CHOICE
8140   GOSUB 8700: REM  BLANK
8150   INVERSE .
8160   GOSUB 8600: REM  THEN DISPLAY IN INVERSE
8170   NORMAL
8180   GOSUB 11400: REM  PAUSE
8190   RETURN
8200 Z = R%(P2): REM  MOVE RIGHT SIDE DOWN/UP ONE
8210   REM  UD = -1 UP, +1 DOWN
8220 R%(P2) = R%(P2 + UD)
8230 R%(P2 + UD) = Z
8300 J = P2: REM  DISPLAY NEW RIGHT J
8310   GOSUB 8900: REM  BLANK
8320   GOSUB 8800: REM  THEN DISPLAY
```

```
8330 J = P2 + UD:P2 = J: REM  MOVE CHOICE
8340  GOSUB 8900: REM  BLANK
8350  INVERSE
8360  GOSUB 8800: REM  THEN DISPLAY IN INVERSE
8370  NORMAL
8380  GOSUB 11400: REM  PAUSE
8390  RETURN
8400 Z = L%(P1): REM  MOVE BOTH SIDES
8410  REM  UD = -1 UP, +1 DOWN
8420 L%(P1) = L%(P1 + UD)
8430 L%(P1 + UD) = Z
8440 Z = R%(P1)
8450 R%(P1) = R%(P1 + UD)
8460 R%(P1 + UD) = Z
8470 J = P1
8480  GOSUB 8700
8490  GOSUB 8900
8500  GOSUB 8800
8510  GOSUB 8800
8520 J = P1 + UD:P1 = J: REM  MOVE ROW
8530  GOSUB 8700
8540  GOSUB 8900
8550  INVERSE
8560  GOSUB 8800
8570  GOSUB 8800
8580  NORMAL
8590  GOTO 11400: REM  PAUSE
8597 :
8598  REM  * DISPLAY ROUTINES *
8599 :
8600 Z$ = L$(L%(J)): REM  DISPLAY LEFT STRING AT ROW J
8610  HTAB HL - LEN (Z$): REM  H-POS
8620  GOTO 8820
8700 Z$ = LEFT$ (BL$,HL - 1): REM  BLANK LEFT STRING AT ROW J
8710  GOTO 8610
8800 Z$ = R$(R%(J)): REM  DISPLAY RIGHT STRING AT ROW J
8810  HTAB HR: REM  H-POS
8820  VTAB V0 + VS * (NR - N + J): REM  ENTRY FOR LEFT STRING
8830  PRINT Z$;
8840  RETURN
8900 Z$ = LEFT$ (BL$,40 - HR): REM  BLANK RIGHT STRING AT ROW J
8910  GOTO 8810
8997 :
8998  REM  ** INSTRUCTIONS **
8999 :
9000  TEXT : HOME
9010  VTAB 4
9020  HTAB 14: PRINT "*** MATCH ***"
9030  PRINT
9040  PRINT
9050  PRINT "THIS IS A MATCHING GAME."
9060  PRINT
9070  PRINT "YOU DECIDE WHICH ITEM ON THE LEFT"
9080  PRINT "MATCHES AN ITEM ON THE RIGHT.  MATCH"
9090  PRINT "THE ITEMS BY TYPING THEIR NUMBERS."
9100  PRINT
9110  PRINT "WHEN YOU MATCH ALL THE ITEMS, YOU WIN."
9120  VTAB 20
9130  PRINT "PRESS ";: INVERSE : PRINT "ESC";: NORMAL : PRINT " TO
   GIVE UP."
9140  PRINT
9150  PRINT "PRESS RETURN TO CONTINUE...";
9160  GOSUB 11500: REM  WAIT FOR KEYSTROKE
9170  IF Z% = - 1 THEN 6100: REM  ESC
9180  RETURN
9497 :
9498  REM  * INITIALIZE THE DISPLAY *
9499 :
9500  HOME
9510  HTAB HC - 2: INVERSE : PRINT "MATCH": NORMAL
9520  FOR K = 1 TO NR: REM  RANDOMLY DISPLAY THE PAIRS
9530 J = INT (NR * RND (1)) + 1: REM  DISPLAY A NEW LEFT PAIR
9540  IF L%(J) > 0 THEN 9530: REM  ALREADY DISPLAYED, TRY AGAIN
9550 L%(J) = - L%(J): REM  FLAG AS DISPLAYED
```

```
9560   GOSUB 8600: REM  DISPLAY LEFT PAIR
9570   J = INT (NR * RND (1)) + 1: REM  NOW DISPLAY A NEW RIGHT PAIR
9580   IF R%(J) > 0 THEN 9570: REM  ALREADY DISPLAYED, TRY AGAIN
9590   R%(J) = - R%(J): REM  FLAG AS DISPLAYED
9600   GOSUB 8800: REM  DISPLAY RIGHT PAIR
9610   NEXT
9620   RETURN
20100   DATA  5,7: REM  INVERTED A
20110   DATA  "1    1"
20120   DATA  "1    1"
20130   DATA  "11111"
20140   DATA  "1    1"
20150   DATA  "1    1"
20160   DATA  " 1 1"
20170   DATA  "  1"
20180   DATA  "-1"
20200   DATA  5,7: REM  INVERTED T
20210   DATA  "  1"
20220   DATA  "  1"
20230   DATA  "  1"
20240   DATA  "  1"
20250   DATA  "  1"
20260   DATA  "  1"
20270   DATA  "11111"
20280   DATA  "-1"
49997  :
49998   REM  ** VARIABLE CONVENTIONS **
49999  :
50000   REM  L$(J)  LEFT STRING OF PAIR (RIGHT JUSTIFIED)
50010   REM  R$(J)  RIGHT STRING OF PAIR (LEFT JUSTIFIED)
50020   REM  L%(J)  LEFT STRING # IN J-TH ROW
50030   REM  R%(J)  RIGHT STRING # IN J-TH ROW
50040   REM  NP     # OF PAIRS
50050   REM  NR     # OF ROWS INITIALLY
50060   REM  N      # OF ROWS LEFT
50070   REM  HL     H-POS + 1 OF RIGHT EDGE OF LEFT COLUMN
50080   REM  HR     H-POS OF LEFT EDGE OF RIGHT COLUMN
50090   REM  HC     H-POS OF CENTER
50100   REM  V0     V-POS OF "ROW 0"
50110   REM  VS     # OF VERTICAL TABS BETWEEN ROWS
50120   REM  BL$    BLANKS
50130   REM  P1     FIRST PICK
50140   REM  P2     SECOND
50990  :
50991  :
50992   REM  ** MATCHING DATA MUST BEGIN AT LINE 51000 **
50993  :
50994   REM  H-POS + 1 OF RIGHT EDGE OF LEFT COLUMN
50995   REM  H-POS OF LEFT EDGE OF RIGHT COLUMN
50996   REM  CONNECTING WORD (MUST FIT BETWEEN COLUMNS)
50997   REM  PAIRS 1,...,NP
50998   REM  END,END
50999  :
51000   DATA  14,27,"MATCHES"
51010   DATA  "ACCELERATE","SPEED UP","FURTIVE","CONCEALED","ZEALOT",
        "HOTHEAD"
51020   DATA  "AUSTERE","STERN","COERCE","COMPEL","MENDACIOUS","LYING"
51030   DATA  "IMPLACABLE","RELENTLESS","TRUCULENT","FIERCE","GRAVE",
        "SOLEMN"
51040   DATA  "PACIFIC","CALM","EXTOL","LAUD","MUNIFICENT","LAVISH"
51050   DATA  "OBDURATE","STUBBORN","INFALLIBLE","PERFECT","INDIGENT",
        "PENURIOUS"
51060   DATA  "INDIGNITY","INSULT","REPLENISH","REFILL","RETICENCE",
        "RESERVE"
51070   DATA  "RELISH","SAVOR","REPRISAL","RETALIATION","IMPROVIDENT",
        "THRIFTLESS"
51080   DATA  "MALADROIT","TACTLESS","IRKSOME","TEDIOUS","TEPID",
        "LUKEWARM"
51090   DATA  "HAMLET","VILLAGE","PLAUDIT","COMMENDATION","CHAGRIN",
        "MORTIFICATION"
51100   DATA  "UBIQUITOUS","OMNIPOTENT","SURMISE","GUESS","MOROSE",
        "GLOOMY"
```

```
51110  DATA   "QUERULOUS","COMPLAINING","TRACTABLE","AMENABLE",
       "ALTERCATION ","QUARREL"
51120  DATA   "HOMILY","SERMON","CRYPTIC","OBSCURE","ADIPOSE","FATTY"
51130  DATA   "DUPLICITY","HYPOCRISY","REGIME","RULE","TENACITY",
       "PERSISTANCE"
51999  DATA   "END","END"
60000  :
60010  REM  * COPYRIGHT 1981 BY HOWARD FRANKLIN, PALO ALTO, CA *
60020  .
```

Merge it with INPUT MODULE, SOUND MODULE (delete lines 18000 through 18999), and IMAGE MODULE. SAVE it as MATCH. RUN it and enjoy.

MATCH makes use of full-screen formatting and inverse video. Although it is entirely text-based, it is an attractive game to watch. MATCH is also designed to be helpful to the player. The relevant instructions remain in view at all times because the text never scrolls out of the text window. Finally the program uses very sophisticated text-moving techniques that make text appear animated (see lines 8000 through 8910).

MATCH is a friendly game and a good example of sound educational design. Error messages are helpful; the right answer receives a more signficant response than the wrong one, and the successful matches remain in view, reinforcing the correct answer. (Incorrectly matched pairs drop to the bottom of the list.)

MATCH makes effective use of the screen. The centered design is both attractive and space-saving. The use of inverse video reinforces the correct answers. Moving the text blocks keeps the player's attention on the screen and the reinforcing value of seeing the matched pairs move and stay together is greater than when lines are drawn (as in a workbook).

Other nice touches in MATCH include the following: The word list is continually renumbered to reflect the number of remaining words, and at the beginning of each new run of the program, words are drawn at random from the DATA pairs and presented in scrambled order.

MATCH can be easily expanded by changing the contents of the DATA statements. However, the greatest power of this program is that it is a completely generalizable matching game. Not only can synonyms be used, but so can any set of text or numeric pairs. Notice in line 51000 that the center word (in this case, MEANS) is in a DATA statement. You can insert states and capitals, equations and their sums, rhyming words or opposites, and, in each case, use a relevant center word.

Below are examples of "win" screens of two possible modifications of MATCH:

CA	CAPITAL	SACRAMENTO
PA	CAPITAL	HARRISBURG
LA	CAPITAL	BATON ROUGE
AZ	CAPITAL	PHOENIX
ME	CAPITAL	PORTLAND
NY	CAPITAL	ALBANY
NE	CAPITAL	LINCOLN

COLT	IS A YOUNG	HORSE
CUB	IS A YOUNG	LION
GOSLING	IS A YOUNG	GOOSE
FAWN	IS A YOUNG	DEER
LAMB	IS A YOUNG	SHEEP
DUCKLING	IS A YOUNG	DUCK
PUPPY	IS A YOUNG	DOG

To use these word matches, replace the DATA statements in lines 51010 through 51999 with new DATA statements that incorporate these words. For example,

```
51010 DATA "CA", "SACRAMENTO", "PA",
"HARRISBURG"
```

You can include as many as fifty pairs of words. The game will randomly select only eight pairs (see line 1300). You may also have to change the center word in line 51000 so that it makes sense with the new words in your current word list.

CHAPTER SUMMARY

This chapter showed three complete text-based games and discussed how to make simple variations to tailor them to your particular audience. The games use the modules presented earlier in the book and exemplify the style and user-friendly attitude we have been discussing all along. The next chapter will give you some even more exciting games that make use of graphics.

CHAPTER SEVEN

Additional Games

This chapter discusses three computer games that incorporate some of the special features introduced earlier in the book.

CONCENTRATION, drawn from the familiar card game of the same name, is an image-based game that lends itself well to the low-resolution graphics of the APPLE. However, this version of CONCENTRATION is entirely new and allows for substantial, yet easy, modification to create various difficulty levels.

STARS is a number-guessing game. The program takes advantage of the computer's quick calculation capabilities. We designed this special version of the game to show off the APPLE's color graphics.

Our version of the popular SIMON game uses sound, LO-RES color, and a scrolling text window.

CONCENTRATION

CONCENTRATION is a solitaire game, although it can be played by several players taking turns. In a typical game, play continues until all the cards are matched. When the game ends, all the cards are displayed face up.

```
10   REM   ...CONCENTRATION-INPUT IMAGE...
11  :
997 :
998   REM   ** ONE-TIME INITIALIZATION **
999 :
1000   DIM PR%(12,1),CD%(24),H%(24),V%(24),CP%(6,1)
1010  MP = 12: REM   MAXIMUM # OF PAIRS OF CARDS
1020  MC = 6: REM                   COLOR PAIRS
1030   REM   MODIFY THE CARD TYPE DISPLAY ROUTINES AT 8300,... IF CH OR
       CV CHANGED!!
1040  CH = 4: REM   HORIZONTAL WIDTH - 1 OF A CARD
1050  CV = 6: REM   VERTICAL HEIGHT - 1
1100   FOR J = 1 TO 24: REM   INITIALIZE CARD LOCATIONS
1110  Z% = (J - 1) / 6
1120  H%(J) = (J - 1 - 6 * Z%) * 6 + 2
1130  V%(J) = Z% * 10
1140   NEXT
1200   DIM BL$(39)
1210  BL$ = ""
1220   FOR J = 1 TO 39
1230  BL$ = BL$ + " "
1240   NEXT
1297 :
1298   REM   * COVER SCREEN *
1299 :
1300   GR : HOME : FOR J = 1 TO 24: GOSUB 8000: NEXT : REM   DISPLAY
       CARDS FACE DOWN
1310  XS = 1:XH = H%(1):XV = V%(1):X$ = "CON":XC(1) = 14: GOSUB 15400
1320  XH = H%(8):XV = V%(8):X$ = "CEN": GOSUB 15400
1330  XH = H%(16):XV = V%(16):X$ = "TRA": GOSUB 15400
1340  XS = 2:XH = H%(20):XV = V%(20):X$ = "TIO": GOSUB 15400
1350  XH = H%(23):X$ = "N": GOSUB 15400
1360   VTAB 23: HTAB 7: PRINT "PRESS RETURN TO CONTINUE...";
1370   GOSUB 11500: REM   WAIT FOR KEYSTROKE
1380   IF Z% = - 1 THEN END : REM   ESC
1497 :
1498   REM   * PARAMETERS FOR THIS GAME *
1499 :
1500  NT = 4: REM   # OF CARD TYPES THIS GAME
1510  NC = 4: REM   # OF COLOR PAIRS
1520  NP = 6: REM   # OF PAIRS OF CARDS
1530  LC$ =  CHR$ ( ASC ("A") - 1 + 2 * NP)
1600   GOSUB 9000: REM   INSTRUCTIONS
1997 :
1998   REM   ** INITIALIZATION FOR NEXT GAME **
1999 :
2000   IF NT * NC < NP THEN   TEXT : HOME : VTAB 11: HTAB 2: PRINT
       "NOT ENOUGH CARDS. CHANGE 1500-1520.": END : REM   * CARDS WILL
       NOT BE UNIQUE *
2010  N = 15
2020   FOR J = 1 TO N: REM   INITIALIZE COLORS
2030  CD%(J) = J
2040   NEXT
2050   GOSUB 2900: REM   SCRAMBLE THE COLORS
2060   FOR J = 1 TO NC: REM   SELECT THE FIRST 2*NC COLORS
2070  CP%(J,0) = CD%(2 * J - 1)
2080  CP%(J,1) = CD%(2 * J)
2090   NEXT
2100  N = NP: REM   # OF CARD PAIRS
2110   FOR J = 1 TO N: REM   INITIALIZE CARD TYPES AND ARRANGEMENTS
2120  PR%(J,0) = NT *  RND (1) + 1: REM   SELECT TYPE FOR PAIR J
2130  PR%(J,1) = NC *  RND (1) + 1: REM   SELECT COLORS FOR PAIR J
2140   IF J = 1 THEN 2200
2150  Z = 0
2160   FOR K = 1 TO J - 1: REM   FORCE PAIR TO BE DIFFERENT FROM
       PREVIOUS PAIRS
2170   IF PR%(J,0) = PR%(K,0) AND PR%(J,1) = PR%(K,1) THEN Z = 1: REM
       SET FLAG FOR SAME PAIR
2180   NEXT
2190   IF Z > 0 THEN 2120: REM   SELECT THE PAIR AGAIN
2200  CD%(2 * J - 1) = J: REM   TWO CARDS FOR PAIR J
2210  CD%(2 * J) = J
2220   NEXT
2230   GOSUB 9500: REM   INITIALIZE THE DISPLAY BEFORE SCRAMBLING
       THE CARDS
2300  N = 2 * NP: REM   # OF CARDS TO BE USED
```

```
2310   GOSUB 2900: REM   SCRAMBLE THE CARDS
2320  TR = 0: REM   # OF TURNS
2400   GOTO 3000
2900   FOR Z = N TO 2 STEP  - 1: REM   SCRAMBLE CD%(1,...,N)
2910  Z% = Z *  RND (1) + 1
2920  Z1 = CD%(Z): REM   EXCHANGE TWO ELEMENTS
2930  CD%(Z) = CD%(Z%)
2940  CD%(Z%) = Z1
2950   NEXT
2960   RETURN
2997  :
2998   REM   ** SELECT NEW PAIR **
2999  :
3000  QP$ = "PICK A CARD: "
3010  QH = 10
3020  P1 = 0: REM   ALLOW ANY VALID PICK
3030   GOSUB 3500: REM   PICK A VALID CARD
3040   IF J = 0 THEN 5200
3050  P1 = J: REM   FIRST PICK
3100  QP$ = "A SECOND: "
3110  QH = 28
3120   GOSUB 3500: REM   PICK ANOTHER VALID CARD
3130   IF J = 0 THEN 5200
3140  P2 = J: REM   SECOND PICK
3150  TR = TR + 1: REM   ONE MORE TURN
3200   VTAB 23: HTAB 10: PRINT  LEFT$ (BL$,30): REM   BLANK PROMPT LINE
3210   IF CD%(P1) (  ) CD%(P2) THEN 4000: REM   CARDS DO NOT MATCH
3220   GOTO 5000: REM   A MATCH
3491  :
3492   REM   * COMMON CODE FOR PICKING CARDS *
3493   REM   ENTRY: QP$ PROMPT
3494   REM          QH  HORIZONTAL TAB FOR PROMPT
3495   REM   EXIT:  J   CARD #
3496   REM             0 ESC
3497   REM   ROUTINE FORCES A NON-MATCHED CARD TO BE SELECTED
3498   REM   DOES NOT ALLOW P1 TO BE PICKED
3499  :
3500   VTAB 23: HTAB QH: PRINT QP$;
3510  YW = 1: GOSUB 10000: REM   INPUT ONE CHARACTER
3520   IF Z% =  - 1 THEN J = 0: RETURN : REM   ESC
3530   IF Z$ ( "A" OR Z$ ) LC$ THEN 3700: REM   LETTER IS NOT IN RANGE
3540  J =  ASC (Z$) -  ASC ("A") + 1
3550   IF CD%(J) (  = 0 OR J = P1 THEN 3600: REM   CARD HAS ALREADY
      BEEN SELECTED
3560   GOSUB 8200: REM   DISPLAY THE CARD
3570   RETURN
3597  :
3598   REM   * ALREADY PICKED *
3599  :
3600  Q$ = "THAT CARD WAS ALREADY PICKED"
3610   GOTO 3710
3697  :
3698   REM   * PICK A VALID LETTER *
3699  :
3700  Q$ = "PICK A LETTER FROM A TO " + LC$
3710  P = 60
3720   GOSUB 3900
3730   GOTO 3500: REM   TRY AGAIN
3891  :
3892   REM   * DISPLAY MESSAGE LINE *
3893  :
3894   REM   ENTRY: Q$  STRING TO DISPLAY
3895   REM          P   PAUSE
3899  :
3900   VTAB 24: HTAB 10: PRINT Q$;
3910   NORMAL
3920  YP = P: GOSUB 11400: REM   PAUSE
3930   HTAB 10: PRINT  LEFT$ (BL$,29);: REM   BLANK MESSAGE LINE
3940   RETURN
3997  :
3998   REM   * CARDS DO NOT MATCH *
3999  :
4000  Q$ = "** NO MATCH **"
4010  P = 150
4020   GOSUB 3900
4100  J = P1: REM   TURN CARD 1 FACE DOWN
```

```
4110   GOSUB 8000
4120   J = P2: REM   TURN CARD 2 FACE DOWN
4130   GOSUB 8000
4140   GOTO 3000: REM   PICK ANOTHER PAIR
4997 :
4998   REM * CARDS MATCH *
4999 :
5000   O$ = "** YOU FOUND A PAIR **"
5010   FLASH
5020   P = 150
5030   GOSUB 3900
5050   J = P1: REM   REMOVE CARD 1
5060   GOSUB 5900
5070   J = P2: REM   REMOVE CARD 2
5080   GOSUB 5900
5100   N = N - 2: REM   TWO LESS CARDS
5110   IF N > 0 THEN 3000: REM   CARDS REMAINING
5200   GR : HOME : REM   DISPLAY THE ORIGINAL BOARD
5210   VTAB 21: INVERSE
5220   IF N > 0 THEN   HTAB 9: INVERSE : PRINT "HERE ARE THE CARDS...":
       NORMAL
5230   IF N = 0 THEN   HTAB 2: PRINT "YOU MATCHED ALL THE PAIRS IN ";TR;
       " TURNS.": NORMAL

5300   FOR J = 1 TO 2 * NP: REM   DISPLAY THE CARDS FACE UP
5310   GOSUB 8200
5320   NEXT
5330   GOTO 6000: REM   AGAIN?
5900   GOSUB 9900: REM   REMOVE CARD J
5910   PRINT " ";
5920   GOSUB 8100: REM   ERASE CARD
5930   CD%(J) =  - CD%(J): REM   FLAG CARD AS MATCHED
5940   RETURN
5997 :
5998   REM ** AGAIN? **
5999 :
6000   HTAB 1: VTAB 24
6010   PRINT "PLAY AGAIN (Y OR N)? ";
6020   GOSUB 11200: REM   Y/N
6030   ON Z% + 2 GOTO 6100,6000,2000,6100: REM   ESC, INVALID, Y, N
6100   PRINT : PRINT
6110   PRINT "THANKS FOR PLAYING.";
6120   END
7997 :
7998   REM * DISPLAY CARDS ROUTINES *
7999 :
8000   COLOR= 1: REM   * DISPLAY CARD J FACE DOWN
8010   GOTO 8110
8100   COLOR= 0: REM   * ERASE CARD J
8110   H = H%(J)
8120   V = V%(J)
8130   FOR Z = H TO H + CH
8140   VLIN V,V + CV AT Z
8150   NEXT
8160   RETURN
8200   Z% =  ABS (CD%(J)): REM   DISPLAY CARD J FACE UP
8210   REM   MODIFY DRAWING ROUTINES IF CH,CV CHANGED
8220   REM   EXIT: Z% PAIR # OF CARD J
8230   H = H%(J): REM   H-POS
8240   V = V%(J): REM   V-POS
8250   C1 = CP%(PR%(Z%,1),0): REM   COLOR 1
8260   C2 = CP%(PR%(Z%,1),1): REM   COLOR 2
8270   ON PR%(Z%,0) GOTO 8300,8400,8500,8600: REM   DISPLAY CARD TYPE
8300   FOR Z = H TO H + 1: REM   TYPE 1 = 3 V-STRIPES
8310   COLOR= C1
8320   VLIN V,V + CV AT Z
8330   VLIN V,V + CV AT Z + 3
8340   NEXT
8350   COLOR= C2
8360   VLIN V,V + CV AT H + 2
8370   RETURN
8400   FOR Z = V TO V + 1: REM   TYPE 2 = 3 H-STRIPES
8410   COLOR= C1
8420   HLIN H,H + CH AT Z
8430   HLIN H,H + CH AT Z + 5
8440   COLOR= C2
8450   HLIN H,H + CH AT Z + 2
```

```
8460    HLIN H,H + CH AT Z + 3
8470    NEXT
8480    RETURN
8500    FOR Z = H TO H + 2 STEP 2: REM   TYPE 3 = 5 V-STRIPES
8510    COLOR= C1
8520    VLIN V,V + CV AT Z
8530    VLIN V,V + CV AT Z + 2
8540    COLOR= C2
8550    VLIN V,V + CV AT Z + 1
8560    NEXT
8570    RETURN
8600    FOR Z = V TO V + 3 STEP 3: REM   TYPE 4 = 5 H-STRIPES
8610    COLOR= C1
8620    HLIN H,H + CH AT Z
8630    HLIN H,H + CH AT Z + 3
8640    COLOR= C2
8650    HLIN H,H + CH AT Z + 1
8660    HLIN H,H + CH AT Z + 2
8670    NEXT
8680    RETURN
8997   :
8998    REM  ** INSTRUCTIONS **
8999   :
9000    TEXT : HOME
9010    PRINT "CONCENTRATION IS A MEMORY GAME."
9020    PRINT
9030    PRINT "PAIRS OF CARDS ARE MIXED UP AND TURNED"
9040    PRINT "OVER.  YOU TRY TO FIND THE PAIRS."
9050    PRINT
9060    PRINT "THE CARDS ARE ARRANGED ACCORDING TO"
9070    PRINT "THIS DIAGRAM:"
9080    INVERSE :Z = 17
9090    HTAB Z: PRINT "ABCDEF"
9100    HTAB Z: PRINT "GHIJKL"
9110    REM   HTAB Z:PRINT "MNOPQR"
9120    REM   HTAB Z:PRINT "STUVWX"
9130    NORMAL
9140    PRINT
9150    PRINT "SELECT A CARD BY TYPING A LETTER FROM A"
9160    PRINT "TO ";LC$;".  (IF YOU WANT THE TOP LEFT CARD,"
9170    PRINT "TYPE A.)"
9180    PRINT
9190    PRINT "YOU MAY SEE ONLY 2 CARDS AT ONE TIME."
9200    PRINT "WHEN YOU MATCH CARDS, THEY DISAPPEAR."
9210    PRINT
9220    PRINT "THERE IS NO GUESS LIMIT."
9230    PRINT
9240    PRINT "PRESS ";: INVERSE : PRINT "ESC";: NORMAL : PRINT
    " TO QUIT."
9250    PRINT
9260    PRINT "PRESS RETURN TO CONTINUE... ";
9270    GOSUB 11500: REM   WAIT FOR KEYSTROKE
9280    IF Z% =  - 1 THEN 6100: REM   ESC
9290    RETURN
9497   :
9498    REM  ** MIXED SCREEN LOWRES SETUP **
9499   :
9500    GR : HOME
9510    FOR J = 1 TO 2 * NP
9520    GOSUB 8000: REM   DISPLAY CARD FACE DOWN
9530    NEXT
9540    VTAB 21: HTAB 10: PRINT "EACH LETTER REPRESENTS A CARD."
9550    HTAB 10: PRINT "TRY TO MATCH THE PAIRS."
9560    INVERSE
9570    FOR J = 1 TO 2 * NP
9580    GOSUB 9900
9590    PRINT  CHR$ ( ASC ("A") - 1 + J);
9600    NEXT
9610    NORMAL
9620    RETURN
9900    Z% = (J - 1) / 6: REM   LOCATE CARD J IN LETTER TEMPLATE
9910    VTAB 21 + Z%
9920    HTAB J - 1 - 6 * Z% + 2
9930    RETURN
49997  :
49998   REM  ** VARIABLE CONVENTIONS **
49999  :
```

```
50000   REM     PR%(J,0) CARD TYPE OF PAIR J
50010   REM     PR%(J,1) COLOR PAIR OF CARD J
50020   REM     CP%(K,0) COLOR 1 OF COLOR PAIR K
50030   REM     CP%(K,1) COLOR 2 OF COLOR PAIR K
50040   REM     CD%(J)   PAIR # OF J-TH CARD IF UNMATCHED
50050   REM              - PAIR # IF ALREADY MATCHED
50060   REM     H%(J)    HORIZONTAL POSITION OF CARD J
50070   REM     V%(J)    VERTICAL
50080   REM     NT       # OF CARD TYPES ACTIVE
50090   REM     NC       # OF COLOR PAIRS ACTIVE
50100   REM     NP       ORIGINAL # OF PAIRS
50110   REM     LC$      LETTER OF LAST CARD
50120   REM     N        # OF CARDS STILL UNMATCHED
50130   REM     CH       HORIZONTAL WIDTH OF A CARD
50140   REM     CV       VERTICAL HEIGHT OF A CARD
50150   REM     TR       # OF TURNS
50160   REM     P1       FIRST PICK
50170   REM     P2       SECOND
60000 :
60010   REM  * COPYRIGHT 1981 BY HOWARD FRANKLIN, PALO ALTO, CA *
60020 :
```

Type it and merge with INPUT MODULE and IMAGE MODULE. SAVE it as CONCENTRATION and RUN it.

In addition to the expected features of the error-trapping input routine, CONCENTRATION incorporates other features that make it easy to use. A matrix of letters at the lower left side of the screen represents the cards. This matrix remains on the screen throughout the game and is updated whenever selections are made and matches found. Thus, a player is reminded not to select the same letter for both cards in a pair and not to select a card that has already been matched. (In the latter case, the clue letter, as well as the card, is removed from the screen.)

What message does the program display when the card selected has already been removed?

— — — — — — — — — —

THAT CARD WAS ALREADY PICKED.
(See Lines 3598 through 3610.)

Another advantage of using the letter matrix is that players don't need to use a joystick or remember a complicated series of directions to move the cursor; all information necessary for playing remains on the screen throughout the game. When a player makes an error, the program prints a helpful message. Players who want to stop the game before the end just press ESC and then RETURN.

Inverse video and flashing text are difficult to use tastefully. However, in CONCENTRATION, inverse is used effectively for the message "YOU MATCHED ALL THE PAIRS." Flash is used to signal that the player found a matching pair.

What line number in the program holds the message that a pair was found?

——————————

Line 5000. Note that Q$ is also used to hold other printed messages at lines 3600, 3700, and 4000 and is always printed at line 3900.

As far as the player is concerned, the game has only one difficulty level. However, you can change several program parameters that affect the game's difficulty. The important items, those that affect what the game looks like, are all written in variables and assigned early in the program. We designed CONCENTRATION so that you can easily change the number and type of color patterns presented. The patterns are combinations of three or five horizontal or vertical stripes (see lines 1040 and 1050). Program changes can make the possibility set include fewer colors (line 1510), fewer stripe variations (line 1500), and more or fewer cards (line 1520). The cards are always scrambled at the beginning of each game.

We chose to display twelve cards (six pairs) and to make the color selection from all color pairs and patterns for aesthetic reasons. We wanted two full rows of cards, and we also wanted a colorful, challenging game. However, you can make your own decisions about those parameters if you make sure that the number of stripe variations times the number of color pairs is greater than, or equal to, the number of pairs of cards.

How do you change the number of cards displayed at the beginning of the game?

————————————

1520 NP = 12 (Twelve is the maximum number of color pairs—see line 1010.)

To make the game easier to play, reduce the number of card pairs, the number of card types and color pairs, and the number of stripes in the cards.

CONCENTRATION has no sound. We think the game should be purely visual. However, if you want to add sound, include SOUND MODULE and assign appropriate numbers to the variables. Many other elegant programming techniques are employed in this game. Look the listing over carefully to find and appreciate them.

STARS

STARS is a number-guessing game originally developed at the People's Computer Center (that later became the Community Computer Center.) Unlike the other number-guessing games, which can just as easily be played with paper and pencil, STARS takes advantage of the computer's quick calculation capability. The program responds to guesses by displaying stars, instead of words, as clues. The more stars you get, the closer you are to the secret number. The program calculates how many stars to display. An interesting feature of STARS is that the response to each guess gives useful information about the correct answer.

STARS was originally written for teletypes. We have written a new, LO-RES color version of it for your APPLE that takes advantage of the APPLE's screen formatting capabilities and also makes use of the error handling in the INPUT MODULE. We have also used the Pause or Keystroke Subroutine. Thus, the program pauses briefly after each clue is displayed, but a player may shorten the pause by pressing a key.

```
10   REM   ...STARS-INPUT SOUND IMAGE...
11   :
997  :
998  REM  ** ONE-TIME INITIALIZATION **
999  :
1000 BP$ =  CHR$ (7)
1010 L2 =  LOG (2)
1020 MN = 1
1030 MX = 40
1040 S1% =  LOG (MX - MN) /  LOG (2) + 1
1050 TB = 13
1060 GB = 38
1070 GT = GB - 27
1197 :
1198  REM  * COVER SCREEN *
1199  :
1200  GR : HOME
1210  FOR Z = 1 TO 100: REM  COLOR DOTS
1220  COLOR= 15: IF  RND (1) < .75 THEN  COLOR= 13
1230  PLOT  INT (40 *  RND (1)),  INT (40 *  RND (1))
1240  NEXT
1250  COLOR= 15: FOR Z = 15 TO 23: REM  WHITE RECTANGLE
1260  HLIN 4,34 AT Z
1270  NEXT
1280  X$ = "STARS":XV = 16:XC(1) = 0:  GOSUB 15300
1290  VTAB 23: HTAB 8:  PRINT "PRESS RETURN TO CONTINUE...";
1300  GOSUB 11500: REM  WAIT FOR KEYSTROKE
1310  IF Z% =  - 1 THEN  END : REM  ESC
1900  GOSUB 9000: REM  INSTRUCTIONS
1997 :
1998  REM  ** INITIALIZATION FOR NEXT GAME **
1999 :
2000  GOSUB 9500: REM  MIXED SCREEN SETUP
2010 A =  INT ((MX - MN + 1) *  RND (1)) + MN
2020 N = 0
2030 YL = MN
2040 YH = MX
2997 :
2998  : REM  ** NEXT TURN **
2999 :
3000  PRINT "GUESS: ";
3010 YW = 3:  GOSUB 11000: REM  INPUT INTEGER
3020  IF Z% =  - 1 THEN 6200: REM  ESC
3030  IF Z% < > 1 THEN  HTAB TB:  PRINT "NUMBER FROM ";MN;" TO ";MX;
     ",  PLEASE": GOTO 3000: REM  INVALID INTEGER
3040 G = Z
3100 N = N + 1: REM  * VALID GUESS *
3110  IF A = G THEN 5000
3997 :
3998  REM  ** INCORRECT GUESS **
3999 :
4000 S% = S1% -  INT ( LOG ( ABS (G - A)) / L2)
4010  GOSUB 8000
4020  GOTO 3000
4997 :
4998  REM  ** CORRECT GUESS **
4999 :
5000 S% = 20
5010  GOSUB 8000: REM  BAR GRAPH
5020 WD = 100:Z$ = "AAHHJJH":  GOSUB 13300: REM  SOUND
5030  PRINT
5040  FLASH
5050  HTAB 9:  PRINT "YOU GOT IT IN ";N;" GUESS";
5060  IF N > 1 THEN  PRINT "ES";
5070  PRINT "!"
5080  NORMAL
5997 :
5998  REM  ** AGAIN? **
5999 :
6000  HTAB 1: VTAB 24
6010  PRINT "PLAY AGAIN (Y OR N)? ";
6020  GOSUB 11200: REM  Y/N
6030  ON Z% + 2 GOTO 6100,6000,2000,6100: REM  ESC, INVALID, Y, N
6100  PRINT : PRINT
6110  PRINT "THANKS FOR PLAYING.";
```

```
6120   END
6197 :
6198   REM  ** QUIT **
6199 :
6200   HTAB TB
6210   PRINT "MY NUMBER WAS ";A
6220   GOTO 6000
7997 :
7998   REM  ** RESPONSE TO GUESS **
7999 :
8000   HTAB TB
8010   SPEED= 120
8020   FOR J = 1 TO S%
8030   PRINT "*";BP$;
8040   NEXT
8050   SPEED= 255
8060   PRINT
8070   IF GB - 3 * S% ( GT THEN S% = S% - 1: GOTO 8070
8100   REM  * PLOT BAR GRAPH *
8110   COLOR= S%
8120   VLIN GB,GB - 3 * S% AT G - MN
8130   RETURN
8997 :
8998   REM  ** INSTRUCTIONS **
8999 :
9000   TEXT : HOME
9010   VTAB 4
9020   HTAB 14: PRINT "*** STARS ***"
9030   PRINT
9040   PRINT
9050   PRINT "I AM THINKING OF A WHOLE NUMBER BETWEEN"
9060   PRINT MN;" AND ";MX;".  TRY TO GUESS WHAT IT IS. "
9070   PRINT
9080   PRINT "AFTER EACH GUESS, I WILL DISPLAY ONE OR"
9090   PRINT "MORE STARS (*).  THE CLOSER YOU ARE TO"
9100   PRINT "MY NUMBER, THE MORE STARS YOU GET."
9110   VTAB 20
9120   PRINT "PRESS ";: INVERSE : PRINT "ESC";: NORMAL : PRINT
       " TO GIVE UP."
9130   PRINT
9140   PRINT "PRESS RETURN TO CONTINUE... ";
9150   GOSUB 11500: REM  WAIT FOR KEYSTROKE
9160   IF Z% =  - 1 THEN 6100: REM  ESC
9200   GR : HOME
9210   I$ = "STARS":XV = 0:XC(1) = 13: GOSUB 15300
9220   PRINT "....5...10...15...20...25...30...35...40"
9230   POKE 34,22: REM  SET SCROLLING WINDOW
9290   RETURN
9497 :
9498   REM  ** MIXED SCREEN LOWRES SETUP **
9499 :
9500   COLOR= 0: FOR Z = GT TO GB: HLIN 0,39 AT Z: NEXT :
       REM  CLEAR GRAPH AREA
9510   HOME : REM  CLEAR SCROLLING WINDOW
9520   RETURN
49991 :
49992  REM  *** STARS ***
49993 :
49994  REM  ORIGINAL VERSION BY PEOPLE'S COMPUTER COMPANY,
       MENLO PARK, CA
49997 :
49998  REM  ** VARIABLE CONVENTIONS **
49999 :
50000  REM     A     ANSWER
50010  REM     BP$   BEEP (CHR$(7))
50020  REM     F     FLAG FOR VALID INPUT
50030  REM     G     GUESS
50040  REM     GB    BOTTOM OF GRAPH
50050  REM     GT    TOP OF GRAPH
50060  REM     J     LOOP COUNTER
50070  REM     L2    LOG(2)
50080  REM     MN    MINIMUM ANSWER
50090  REM     MX    MAXIMUM
50100  REM     N     # OF GUESSES
50110  REM     S%    # OF STARS FOR GUESS
50120  REM     S1%   MAX # OF STARS + 1
```

```
50130  REM    TB   TAB POSITION FOR RESPONSE
60000  :
60010  REM  * COPYRIGHT 1981 BY HOWARD FRANKLIN, PALO ALTO, CA *
60020  :
```

Type it and merge with INPUT MODULE, SOUND MODULE, (delete lines 18000 through 19999) and IMAGE MODULE. SAVE it as STARS and RUN it.

As you remember, LO-RES permits only four lines of text at the bottom of the screen, so we put the instructions at the beginning of the program. However, the visual display reminds the players of the game's idea.

In STARS, the clues are dramatically displayed on the LO-RES screen. The number line provides a visual organization of the information that simply was not available in the teletype game. Because all clues remain in view, we think it is acceptable to leave only one previous response in the text portion of the screen.

This version of STARS is particularly pleasing to us because we have integrated the graphics into the game, rather than using them simply as decorations. When you are designing or enhancing your own programs, try to consider how you can integrate graphics, using lines and images to display helpful information.

We did not limit the number of guesses permitted as is usually done in games of this type. Limiting the number of guesses in an easy game can inhibit play by children. Using the ESC convention to let the player choose to quit is much more friendly.

SIMON

SIMON is our version of the popular game in which the computer plays a tune and the player tries to play back the same tune.

```
10   REM  ...SIMON-INPUT SOUND...
11  :
997 :
998   REM  ** ONE-TIME INITIALIZATION **
999 :
1000  DIM T%(30)
1100  Q1 = 1: REM  ECHO DIGIT IN TUNE OPTION
1110  Q2 = 1: REM  NOTE UNDER BOX OPTION
1120  Q3 = 1: REM  SELECT BOX OPTION
1130  Q4 = 1: REM  SOUND NOTE OPTION
1200  TL = 1: REM  LOWEST NOTE
1210  TH = 8: REM  HIGHEST NOTE
1220  TD = 80: REM  DURATION OF EACH NOTE
1230  TP = 10: REM  PAUSE BETWEEN SOUNDS
1240  LL = 3: REM  MINIMUM LENGTH OF TUNE
1250  LH = 20: REM  MAXIMUM
1300  BV = 3: REM  BOX HEIGHT
1310  VR = 30: REM  V-POS OF BOX AT REST
1320  VS = VR - BV - 8: REM  V-POS OF BOX SELECTED
1330  HT = 19: REM  H-POS OF TUNE
1340  VC = 23: REM  V-POS OF COMPUTER'S TUNE
1350  VL = 24: REM  V-POS OF LENGTH
1360  VY = 22: REM  V-POS OF YOUR TUNE
1400  CB = 1: REM  BACKGROUND COLOR
1410  CR = 2: REM  BOX AT REST COLOR
1420  CR = 3: REM  BOX SELECTED COLOR
1500  L = LL: REM  LENGTH OF FIRST TUNE
1597 :
1598  REM  * COVER SCREEN *
1599 :
1600  TEXT : HOME
1610 WP = 0: GOSUB 13000: REM  AVOID INITIALIZATION DELAY WITH FIRST
     NOTE
1620 S$ = "SIMON"
1630  FOR J = 1 TO  LEN (S$)
1640  VTAB 16: HTAB 17 + J: INVERSE : PRINT  MID$ (S$,J,1)
1650  VTAB 12 - 2 * J: HTAB 2 + 6 * J: PRINT  MID$ (S$,J,1);: NORMAL
1660 WP = J:WD = 60: GOSUB 13000: REM  NOTE J
1670 YP = 15: GOSUB 11400: REM  AUSE
1680  PRINT CHR$ (8);" "
1690  NEXT
1700 ·SPEED= 100: FOR Z = 1 TO 4: PRINT  CHR$ (7);: NEXT : SPEED= 255
1710  VTAB 23: HTAB 8: PRINT "PRESS RETURN TO CONTINUE...";
1720  GOSUB 11500: REM  WAIT FOR KEYSTROKE
1730  IF Z% =  - 1 THEN END : REM  ESC
1900  REM  GOSUB 9000: REM INSTRUCTIONS
1997 :
1998  REM  ** INITIALIZATION FOR NEXT TUNE **
1999 :
2000  FOR J = 1 TO L: REM  GENERATE TUNE
2010 T%(J) = (TH - TL) *  RND (1) + TL
2020  NEXT
2030  GOSUB 8300: REM  SET UP BOXES
2040 VT = VC:Q9 = Q1:Q1 = 0: GOSUB 8900: REM  PLAY COMPUTER'S TUNE
     (DO NOT PRINT TUNE)
2050 Q1 = Q9: REM  RESTORE PRINT TUNE OPTION
2060 YP = 10: GOSUB 11400: REM  PAUSE
2100  HOME
2110  VTAB VL: HTAB HT - 8: PRINT "LENGTH: ";L;: REM  DISPLAY LENGTH
2120  VTAB VY: HTAB HT - 11: PRINT "YOUR TUNE:";
2130 NJ = 1: REM  FIRST NOTE
2997 :
2998  REM  ** GET NEXT NOTE IN TUNE **
2999 :
3000  GOSUB 11600: REM  GET KEYSTROKE, NO ECHO, WITH TYPE-AHEAD
3010  IF Z% =  - 1 THEN  VTAB VY: HTAB HT - 1 + NJ: FLASH : PRINT
     "ESC";: NORMAL : GOTO 4000: REM  ESC
3020 N = Z - 176: REM  CONVERT TO NOTE #
3030  IF N < TL OR N > TH THEN 3000: REM  INVALID NOTE
3040 VT = VY: GOSUB 8600: REM  RESPOND TO NOTE
3050  IF N = T%(NJ) THEN 5000: REM  CORRECT NOTE
3997 :
3998  REM  ** TUNE WAS INCORRECT **
3999 :
4000  SPEED= 100: FOR Z = 1 TO 4: PRINT  CHR$ (7);: NEXT : SPEED= 255
4010 YP = 10: GOSUB 11400: REM  PAUSE
```

```
4020 Q9 = Q1:Q1 = 1: GOSUB 8800: REM  PLAY COMPUTER'S TUNE (PRINT
     TUNE)
4030 Q1 = Q9: REM  RESTORE PRINT TUNE OPTION
4040  IF L > LL THEN L = L - 1
4050  GOTO 6000: REM  AGAIN?
4997 :
4998  REM ** CORRECT NOTE **
4999 :
5000 NJ = NJ + 1
5010  IF NJ < = L THEN 3000: REM  NEXT NOTE
5097 :
5098  REM ** GOT IT **
5099 :
5100  HOME
5110  VTAB VY: HTAB HT - 12: PRINT "YOU GOT IT: ";
5120 Q9 = Q1:Q1 = 1: GOSUB 8800: REM  PLAY THE TUNE (PRINT TUNE)
5130 Q1 = Q9: REM  RESTORE PRINT TUNE OPTION
5140  REM ** NEXT TUNE IS ONE LONGER **
5150  IF L < LH THEN L = L + 1
5997 :
5998  REM ** AGAIN? **
5999 :
6000  HTAB 1: VTAB 24
6010  PRINT "ANOTHER TUNE (Y OR N)? ";
6020  GOSUB 11200: REM  Y/N
6030  ON Z% + 2 GOTO 6100,6000,2000,6100: REM  ESC, INVALID, Y, N
6100  PRINT : PRINT
6110  PRINT "THANKS FOR PLAYING.";
6120  END
7997 :
7998  REM ** DISPLAY BOX SUBROUTINES **
7999 :
8000  COLOR= CR: REM  * DISPLAY BOX N AT REST
8010 Z = VR
8020  GOTO 8200
8050  COLOR= CB: REM  * ERASE BOX N AT REST
8060  GOTO 8010
8100  COLOR= CS: REM  * DISPLAY BOX N SELECTED
8110 Z = VS
8120  GOTO 8200
8150  COLOR= CB: REM  * ERASE BOX N SELECTED
8160  GOTO 8110
8200 Z1 = - 4 + 5 * N: REM  * DISPLAY BOX N AT ROW Z
8210  REM  N = BOX #
8220  REM  COLOR SET FOR DISPLAY OR ERASE
8230  REM  Z = ROW #
8240  FOR Z2 = Z + BV - 1 TO Z STEP - 1: REM  DISPLAY FROM BOTTOM
8250  HLIN Z1,Z1 + 2 AT Z2
8260  NEXT
8270  RETURN
8300  GR : HOME : REM  * DISPLAY BACKGROUND AND INITIAL BOXES
8310  COLOR= CB
8320  FOR Z = 0 TO 38
8330  HLIN 0,39 AT Z
8340  NEXT
8350  FOR N = TL TO TH
8360  GOSUB 8000
8370  NEXT
8380  RETURN
8400 Z$ = STR$ (N): REM  * ECHO DIGIT UNDER BOX N
8410  INVERSE
8420  GOTO 8500
8450 Z$ = " ": REM  * ERASE DIGIT UNDER BOX N
8500  VTAB 21: REM  * DISPLAY Z$ UNDER BOX N
8510  HTAB - 2 + 5 * N
8520  PRINT Z$;
8530  NORMAL
8540  RETURN
8600  REM  * RESPOND TO NOTE N, NJ NOTE IN TUNE, ECHO NOTE ON LINE VT
8610  IF Q1 > 0 THEN  VTAB VT: HTAB HT - 1 + NJ: INVERSE : PRINT N;:
     NORMAL : REM  ECHO NOTE IN TUNE
8620  IF Q2 > 0 THEN  GOSUB 8400: REM  ECHO NOTE UNDER BOX
8630  IF Q3 > 0 THEN  GOSUB 8050: GOSUB 8100: REM  SELECT BOX
8640  IF Q4 > 0 THEN  WD = TD:WP = N: GOSUB 13000: REM  PLAY NOTE
8650 YP = TP: GOSUB 11400: REM  PAUSE
8660  IF Q3 > 0 THEN  GOSUB 8150: GOSUB 8000: REM  DE-SELECT BOX
```

```
8670  IF Q2 > 0 THEN  GOSUB 8450: REM  ERASE NOTE UNDER BOX
8680  RETURN
8800  VT = VC: REM  * PLAY THE COMPUTER'S TUNE
8810  IF Q1 > 0 THEN  VTAB VT: HTAB HT - 17: PRINT "COMPUTER'S TUNE:";
8900  REM  * PLAY TUNE ON LINE VT *
8910  FOR NJ = 1 TO L
8920  N = T%(NJ)
8930  GOSUB 8600: REM  RESPOND TO NOTE NJ IN TUNE
8940  NEXT
8950  RETURN
8997  :
8998  REM  ** INSTRUCTIONS **
8999  :
9000  TEXT : HOME
9200  PRINT
9210  PRINT "PRESS ";: INVERSE : PRINT "ESC";: NORMAL : PRINT
      " TO QUIT."
9220  PRINT
9230  PRINT "PRESS RETURN TO CONTINUE... ";
9240  GOSUB 11500
9250  IF Z% = - 1 THEN 6100: REM  ESC
9260  RETURN
13120  DATA  255,228,203,192,171,152,135,127
60000  :
60010  REM  * COPYRIGHT 1981 BY HOWARD FRANKLIN, PALO ALTO, CA *
60020  :
```

Type it and merge with INPUT MODULE and SOUND MODULE. SAVE it as SIMON and RUN it.

The player's task is to copy the computer's tune, using the number keys. Our game provides both visual and auditory clues—the blocks move and the numbers appear as the note sounds. The player can concentrate on the numbers, the relative position of the blocks, the notes, or any combination of these three.

Look at all the variables you can change to alter the game (see lines 1100 through 1500). Changing these variables gives this game a tremendous range of possible variations! To minimize visual distraction, we have colored all blocks the same color. You can change the box color and background color by changing the colors in lines 1400, 1410, and 1420.

Each successive tune is different, created at random from the available notes. The difficulty of the game is determined only by the tune's length. Longer tunes are more difficult; shorter tunes are easier. The player's success with the previous tune determines whether the next tune will be harder or easier. Thus, the game constantly adjusts itself to match the player's ability.

You can also make the game more difficult by shortening the pause between notes. What line number would you change?

——————————

1230 TP=

The number of possible notes (and of blocks in the game) is determined in the program. We have used eight notes.
1.   How would you modify the program to make it select from only five notes?

2.   How do you change the length of the first tune played to 5?

3.   How would you modify the program to eliminate the numbers that appear when a note is played?

——————————

1.   1210 TH = 5 (Or change TL and TH so that any five numbers separate them.)
2.   1240 LL = 5
3.   1110 Q2 = 0

The program responds immediately to the first incorrectly pressed key. Thus, if a tune is 3 5 4, and you type 3 6 4, the program will stop at the 6, signal you, and play the tune correctly.

CHAPTER SUMMARY

This chapter is our pride and joy. In it we have shown you three superlative games. STARS is a high-tech version of an old computer standard; CONCENTRATION and SIMON are popular games from other media. In these versions we have brought them into the space age. With the many easy-to-make variations, you have a myriad of possible CONCENTRATION and SIMON games. Enjoy them all!

APPENDIX A

Renumber/Append Routine

To easily use the routines and subroutines provided in this book, you must merge the routines with your own programs. In some cases, you will have to renumber your programs so the merge can take place.

On the System Master disk that came with your APPLE computer is a utility program that allows you to both renumber and append (merge) programs. Here is a brief summary of how to use the program (a complete set of instructions can be viewed by running the program called RENUMBER INSTRUCTIONS).

1. RUN the RENUMBER program. It will be loaded and saved in the high memory locations of the computer.
2. Load your program into memory by typing: LOAD NAME1 RETURN
3. Type: &H RETURN. Your program will be placed on HOLD.
4. Load the second program by typing: LOAD NAME2 RETURN
5. Merge the two programs together by typing: &M RETURN. The resulting program will be found in memory. You should SAVE it using its own name before you do anything else (better safe than sorry). The complete program can now be RUN.

We have intentionally numbered our routines and subroutines so that they should not interfere with programs you will write. It is important that the line numbers of the two programs you want to merge do not overlap. If they do, some strange things will occur. For example, if two statements have the same line number, they will both appear in the final program. To avoid this and other problems, you should renumber the statements in your program and/or the subroutine you wish to merge so line numbers do not overlap. You can use the same RENUMBER program described above. The procedure is:

1. RUN the RENUMBER program to save it in high memory.
2. Load the program to be renumbered.
3. To renumber your program type: & RETURN. Your entire program will be renumbered starting with line ten in increments of ten. All line number references in GOTO, GOSUB, IN..GOTO, and IF..THEN statements will be fixed for you. It may take as much as one minute to completely renumber a 16K program. Your computer will be sitting idle, but don't panic and hit RESET. This program may now be SAVEd, RUN, LISTed, or anything else.

The renumber process can also renumber starting with a number other than ten, or in increments other than ten. You can also use the program to renumber segments of programs without renumbering the entire program. Here is the explanation:

F indicates the first new line number.
I indicates the increment between lines.
S is the start or first line number to be renumbered.
E is the last or ending line number to be renumbered.

&F 100, I 20, S 350, E 660—Renumber the statements between 350 and 660 in increments of 20, beginning with line 100. The resulting line numbers will be 100, 120, 140, . . .

&S 1000, E 2500, F 1000, I 15—Renumber the statements from 1000 to 2500 beginning with line 1000 and incrementing by 15. The resulting line numbers will be 1000, 1015, 1030. . . .

Appendix B

Random Ramblings From One Programmer to Another

This appendix, written for the experienced programmer, outlines the rationale behind some of the programming choices made throughout this book. It describes the need for a subroutine library and the restrictions in APPLESOFT BASIC that affect the construction and use of such a library. Assembly listings are included for those features that are essential but cannot be written in BASIC. This appendix is also a collection of comments about some of the programs presented that are too technical to present elsewhere (also known as "ramblings").

This appendix, however, is by no means a thorough, step-by-step analysis and description of each algorithm and line of code. The REMs contained within the listings trace the flow and can be studied to answer specific questions.

Subroutine Library

From a program design viewpoint, a subroutine extends the capability of a given programming language. Once constructed and debugged, a subroutine is logically equivalent to a "super-command." Some subroutines are specific "super-commands" for a given application (i.e., display a variable number of *'s in STARS, line 8000). Other subroutines are more general "super-commands" that are useful in many applications (i.e., input and echo a string, trap for ESC, and test if it is an integer within a variable range). A subroutine library is simply a collection of those subroutines which are considered to be of general use.

This book has developed four subroutine modules (groupings of subroutines). Each module extends the capabilities of APPLESOFT. INPUT MODULE extends the INPUT/GET commands, SOUND MODULE implements a sound function. IMAGE MODULE manipulates block images in LO-RES graphics, and NEXTDATA MODULE implements a RESTORE to any line number, rather than to the first DATA statement. Refer to chapter summaries for their usage. Ramblings about these modules appear later in this appendix.

Problems in Implementing a Subroutine Library

There are two types of problems to solve when implementing a subroutine library. The first type involves limitations imposed by the given programming language. In APPLESOFT, there are three: variable name conflicts (changing values of variables in the subroutines that are also used in the main program), line-number conflicts (overlapping ranges of line numbers), and DATA-statement conflicts (inability to READ data from a given line number because DATA statements from other subroutines, or even the main program itself, might precede it). Other programming languages, or even other versions of BASIC, eliminate some or all of these "syntactical" problems. LOCAL variables eliminate the first; languages without line numbers eliminate the second (obviously not BASIC); and "RESTORE X," where X is a line number, eliminates the third.

The second type of problem in implementing a subroutine library involves difficulty in actual use of the library. "Calling sequences" (where, with what entry conditions, and with what exit conditions) must be clearly documented. Initialization requirements must also be specified (i.e., "Load machine code routine X at location Y before using"). Most important, the subroutines themselves should be well-modularized, avoiding unnecessary "side-effects" (i.e., displaying "OUT OF RANGE"), so that they are usable in a variety of applications. All of these problems are generally independent of a given programming language. Instead, they are a function of careful planning by the programmer.

Solutions Chosen

There is no "right answer" to these problems. Instead, there are a variety of solutions which will work. Those presented in this book are "best choices" made by the programmer for various objective and subjective reasons (ease of interfacing, aesthetics, and whims).

Problem #1: Variable-Name Conflicts

By fiat, variable names beginning with W are reserved for the SOUND MODULE, X for IMAGE MODULE, Y for INPUT MODULE and NEXTDATA MODULE, and Z as temporary variables. In general, main programs should only use variable names beginning with A/V.

This solution may at first seem arbitrary since not many of the possible variable names in the range W/Z are used in the modules. An alternative might be to select a small, reusable set, and document the actual "reserved" names. This solution is not "easy" or "aesthetic" for various reasons: It is easier to remember not to use W/Z than not to use certain reserved names; it is more difficult to ensure that the modules themselves do not conflict with each other; it is more difficult to interface with the modules when "obscure" variable names are used. BASIC code is hard enough to read, anyway, and variable names were selected to preserve mnemonics where possible (i.e., XH is a horizontal position for the IMAGE MODULE, while YH is the highest integer in the range in the INPUT MODULE—YM could be minimum or maximum). The proposed solution generates prettier code.

Following are some additional prejudices about variable names. Avoid the letters I and O—they are too easily confused with 1 and 0. By convention, use integer variables for return codes (Z%=−1 ESC; =0 invalid integer; =1 valid integer), not for return values (Z=value if integer valid). Also use integer variables for flags (WR%>0 if sound routine already loaded). To conserve RAM, use integer arrays, rather than real arrays, where possible (i.e., L%() and R%() in MATCH). Use INT() rather than integer variable—the code is easier to follow.

No consideration has been given to improving execution time of the programs by ordering the appearance of variables. (Refer to *APPLESOFT II Reference Manual*, Appendix E.) There is no unobscure way to include this capability in a subroutine library; however, the experienced programmer may play at will. The programmer chose program clarity as more important and so chose to ignore the speed-of-execution issue. With the exception of IMAGE MODULE, the subroutines run "fast enough."

Problem #2: Line Number Conflicts

By fiat, reserve lines 10xxx/11xxx for INPUT MODULE, lines 13xxx for SOUND MODULE, lines 15xxx for IMAGE MODULE, lines 19xxx for NEXTDATA MODULE, and lines 20100/49999 for the image library in IMAGE MODULE.

As with the variable name solution, this solution also has competition. An alternative is to use the Renumber Program not only for merging (as it is now used to append subroutines to the main program) but for renumbering as well—simply renumber the subroutines needed where there is "room." The major objection to this solution is that the entry points will vary from program to program and will therefore be more difficult to use than fixed-entry points. Further, it seems as though there are enough line numbers left for the main program. The programmer's aesthetics require modules to begin on 10000—boundaries, major logical portions on 1000—boundaries, and minor portions on 100—boundaries. Therefore, massive renumbering leaves the program harder to follow (and ugly).

GOTOs and GOSUBs are never to lines containing only REMs, in case they are deleted or left out when typing. Subroutines should be entered at the beginning—tricky entrances in the middle are dangerous and make the code difficult to modify later (restructuring subroutine nesting/entry variables can eliminate this need).

One of the goals in making the listings readable was to select variable names, line numbering, and REM usage that was reasonably consistent from program to program (i.e., make the programs look like each other). The programmer's aesthetics evolved during this process with the effect that later programs are more consistent than earlier ones ("It's too hard to be consistent"). It's difficult to write pretty code in BASIC; these programs represent one programmer's attempts to create beauty.

As with ordering the appearance of variables, carefully ordering line numbers can speed up execution (see *APPLESOFT II Reference Manual*, Appendix E). Likewise for the reasons to ignore this problem.

Problem #3: DATA Statement Conflicts

The solution is straightforward and tricky. A "RESTORE X" (where X is any line number) was added in NEXTDATA MODULE. Many BASIC's already have this capability—unfortunately, APPLESOFT does not. The image library in IMAGE MODULE avoids an incredible amount of bookkeeping by beginning each image at 20000+100*# and is easily implemented with RESTORE X. SOUND MODULE loads machine code routines by POKEing from DATA statements, rather than individual POKEs. (Notice, however, that NEXTDATA MODULE must load its machine code with POKEs.)

Here is an assembly listing of RESTORE X:

```
                  6       *
                  7       * APPLESOFT EQUATES
                  8       *
                  9       DATPTR    EQU    $7D ;MEMORY LOCATION FOR
                NEXT READ
                 10       LINNUM    EQU    $50 ;LINE NUMBER FOR 'FNDLIN'
                 11       LOWPTR    EQU    $9B ;ADDRESS FROM 'FNDLIN'
                 12       FNDLIN    EQU    $D61A ;SEARCH FOR LINE NUMBER
                 13       *
                 14       *
                 15       * RESTOREX - NEXT READ FROM LINE X
                 16       *
                 17       LINEX     DS     2 ;LINE NUMBER
                 18       *
0302:  AD 00 03   19       RESTOREX  LDA    LINEX ;SET LINNUM
0305:  85 50      20                 STA    LINNUM
0307:  AD 01 03   21                 LDA    LINEX+1
030A:  85 51      22                 STA    LINNUM+1
030C:  20 1A D6   23                 JSR    FNDLIN ;SEARCH
030F:  A5 9B      24                 LDA    LOWPTR ;UPDATE POINTER FOR
                NEXT READ
0311:  18         25                 CLC
0312:  69 04      26                 ADC    #4 ;OFFSET FOR ACTUAL DATA
0314:  85 7D      27                 STA    DATPTR
0316:  A5 9C      28                 LDA    LOWPTR+1
0318:  69 00      29                 ADC    #0
031A:  85 7E      30                 STA    DATPTR+1
031C:  60         31                 RTS
```

Problem #4: Documenting Calling Sequences

The chapter summaries include all the calling sequences for each module. Additionally, REMs precede each entry point in the listings. If REMs must be deleted to save space, the entry point REMs should be deleted last.

Problem #5: Initialization Requirements

The modules are self-initializing. They work even if the program "forgets" to initialize them. This was an important design goal since novice programmers are encouraged to use the modules in their programs.

The solution is a rare example of an APPLESOFT trick (i.e., "It won't necessarily work in other BASICs") that the programmer could stomach. (The programmer finds that tricks, or "kludges" interfere with proper digestion.) This solution relies on the "feature" that RUN sets all arithmetic variables to 0 and sets strings to empty. Wherever initialization is required, a flag is tested (i.e., SOUND MODULE, line 13000 WR%=0 not initialized; >0 already initialized). See INPUT MODULE, line 10000 for initializing YF$, the filler character. See IMAGE MODULE, lines 15310 and 15410 for initializing XS, the space between images. Line 15020 in IMAGE MODULE (relying on an automatic DIM XC(10)) represents a marginally acceptable juggling of the programmer's aesthetics ("Why not?")

Problem #6: Well Modularized,
Avoiding Unnecessary "Side-Effects"

The programmer thinks so and the publisher has been explicitly instructed not to represent opposing points of view.

SELECTED COMMENTS ABOUT THE PROGRAMS

The sound chapter uses two machine code routines, one to produce pitches for a fixed duration (SOUND), and the other to produce pitches until a new key is pressed (ORGAN). Assembly listings are included below:

```
              33     *
              34     * APPLESOFT EQUATES
              35     *
              36     CLICK       EQU    $C030 ;SPEAKER TOGGLE
              37     *
              38     *
              39     * SOUND - SOUND A PITCH FOR A SET DURATION
              40     *
              41     * ENTRY  : DURATION-L,H SET
              42     *          1: PITCH  OFFSET IN 'PITCHTBL' (1/40)
              43     *          2: PITCH  SET
              44     *
              45     DURATION    DS     2
              46     PITCH       DS     1
              47     *
              48     * ENTRY 1: USE 'PITCH' AS OFFSET TO ACTUAL
                   PITCH
0320: AC 1F 03 49   SOUND1      LDY    PITCH
0323: B9 49 03 50               LDA    PITCHTBL-1,Y
0326: 8D 1F 03 51               STA    PITCH
              52     *
              53     * ENTRY 2: 'PITCH' SET
0329: A0 00    54   SOUND2      LDY    #0 ;INITIALIZE 24-BIT
                   "COUNTER"
032B: EE 1D 03 55               INC    DURATION
032E: EE 1E 03 56               INC    DURATION+1
              57     *
0331: AE 1F 03 58   NXTCLICK    LDX    PITCH ;RESTORE PITCH COUNT
0334: AD 30 C0 59               LDA    CLICK ;"CLICK" SPEAKER
              60     *
0337: 88       61   COUNTDOWN   DEY    ;24-BIT COUNTER
                   (Y, DURATION-L,H)
0338: D0 0A    62               BNE    NOTDONE
033A: CE 1D 03 63               DEC    DURATION
033D: D0 05    64               BNE    NOTDONE
033F: CE 1E 03 65               DEC    DURATION+1
0342: F0 05    66               BEQ    DONE
              67     *
0344: CA       68   NOTDONE     DEX    ;CHECK IF NEXT CLICK YET
0345: F0 EA    69               BEQ    NXTCLICK
0347: D0 EE    70               BNE    COUNTDOWN
              71     *
0349: 60       72   DONE        RTS
              73     *
              74     * PITCHTBL - PITCH VALUES
034A: FF F2 E4 75   PITCHTBL    HEX    FFF2E4D7CBC0B5AB ;1/8
0352: A1 98 8F 76               HEX    A1988F877F78716B ;9/16
035A: 65 5F 5A 77               HEX    655F5A55504B4743 ;17/24
0362: 3F 3B 38 78               HEX    3F3B3835322F2C2A ;25/32
036A: 28 25 23 79               HEX    28252321201E1C1A ;33/40

              81     *
              82     * APPLESOFT EQUATES
              83     *
              84     KEY         EQU    $C000
              85     *
              86     *
              87     * ORGAN - SOUND A PITCH UNTIL ANY KEY IS
                   PRESSED
              88     *
              89     * ENTRY: PITCH  OFFSET IN 'PITCHTBL' (1/40)
              90     *
0372: AC 1F 03 91   ORGAN       LDY    PITCH
0375: B9 49 03 92               LDA    PITCHTBL-1,Y
0378: 8D 1F 03 93               STA    PITCH
037B: AD 00 C0 94   ORGCLICK    LDA    KEY ;CHECK KEYBOARD
037E: 30 0E    95               BMI    ORGDONE ;-> KEY WAS PRESSED
0380: AE 1F 03 96               LDX    PITCH ;RESTORE PITCH COUNT
0383: AD 30 C0 97               LDA    CLICK ;"CLICK" SPEAKER
              98     *
              99     * THE NEXT TWO INSTRUCTIONS ARE INCLUDED TO
                   MAKE
             100     * THE TIMING OF THE "INNER LOOP" APPROXIMATELY
                   EQUAL
             101     * TO THAT OF THE PREVIOUS ROUTINE 'SOUND'.
             102     *
```

```
               103   * THIS RESULTS IN THE PITCH VALUES PRODUCING
                       SIMILAR
               104   * PITCHES IN EACH ROUTINE
               105   *
0386:  88      106   ORGCOUNT   DEY
0387:  D0 00   107              BNE    ORGNOP
               108   ORGNOP     EQU    *  ;END OF "WASTE" TIME
0389:  CA      109              DEX       ;CHECK IF NEXT CLICK YET
038A:  F0 EF   110              BEQ    ORGCLICK
038C:  D0 F8   111              BNE    ORGCOUNT
               112   *
038E:  60      113   ORGDONE    RTS
```

Notice that SOUND has two entries. The first, SOUND1, uses PITCH to look up a value in PITCHTBL. The second, SOUND2, uses PITCH as the actual value. Sounds are produced by clicking the speaker at an internal frequency determined by the value in PITCH. The relationship of the internal frequency to actual sound is a function of the timing of the machine code. Notice that PITCHTBL has allocated space for forty different internal frequencies. The 16-bit value in DURATION controls the length of the sound.

ORGAN uses the same frequencies in PITCHTBL and "wastes time" in its internal loop so that the internal timings approximate those of SOUND. Unlike DURATION in SOUND, ORGAN continues to produce its tone until a key is pressed. One of the limitations of the APPLE hardware is that there is no way to detect when a key has been released. Therefore, ORGAN must wait for a new key press to terminate.

In the LO-RES Chapter, INPUT LENGTHS segments the keyboard into different sections, with each section affecting a different internal parameter. This technique might be applicable to one of your programs and a simple addition to INPUT MODULE will implement it.

The elegance of a subroutine library can be seen in the addition of three BASIC commands to SPIRAL2 to create SPIRAL SOUND. (The LO-RES cover screens in the last two chapters are also added with minimal new code.)

IMAGE MODULE is already discussed in some detail in its chapter. Worth mentioning here is that execution speed can be substantially increased with the addition of machine code routines. This is, however, not the purpose of the book. Machine code was used only in the absence of a BASIC solution. Program length/disk access time can be shortened by including only those images you need in your program.

As for HI-RES, the programmer is thankful that there are commercial packages available The APPLE hardware can do it, but APPLE-SOFT is another matter. Refer to the *APPLESOFT Reference Manual* if the numeric variables and arrays (or even the program) override the HI-RES screen buffers—Appendix L contains the Zero Page pointers that can verify whether this has occurred.

INPUT MODULE traps for the ESC key since it provides one of the few special keys that can be used by program logic to exit from the current level in a game (i.e., program). Requiring ESC-RETURN and echoing ESC eliminates the problem of a "hot" ESC key.

ONERRGOTO is essentially useless, except while debugging programs. Errors 0/224 are errors in logic (program redesign can avoid them). Since INPUT MODULE does not use the INPUT command, error 254 is not possible. Error 255, CTRL-C, is a nice idea but was incorrectly implemented—execution RESUMEs with the statement that was just executed (i.e., RESUME after a CTRL-C will re-execute the same instruction, rather than continuing with the next). Alas, CTRL-C is only trapped while waiting for input. It is fatal if pressed otherwise. Maybe error 255 could be used to display a graceful *adieu* before the demise. Even if a brilliant solution is discovered, the user still has the RESET (or, CTRL-RESET) key in his arsenal.

STORY is an example of a simple game gone wild with a cover screen in LO-RES, a trap for word breaks when displaying, and DATA-driven questions and story construction.

BLOCKOUT struggled to overcome limitations in APPLESOFT substrings. The SCRN function, omitted from discussion in the LO-RES chapter, is used in line 8350 to guarantee that the block changes to a new color.

Both MATCH and CONCENTRATION have fun manipulating data structures and produce some fascinating visual effects. Notice the addition of an inverted A and an inverted T to the IMAGE library for the MATCH cover screen. As an added challenge, play CONCEN-TRATION on a black and white TV and try distinguishing the subtle variations.

STARS was another old favorite that got out of hand with the addition of LO-RES and sound. The effect of the graph erasing itself was purely accidental.

SIMON reminds your programmer of the hot dog stands that advertize 1,048,576 varieties. The programs minimize the use of monitor calls and ESC sequences in PRINT comands. Such features obscure the readability of programs. A better solution is for language designers to expand languages to include additional commands (i.e., HOME instead of CALL-936). Until then, your programmer prefers to PRINT a string of blanks, rather than to CALL a monitor routine that clears to the end of the line.

Please Write

Your programmer welcomes all correspondence but regrets, in advance, that there may not be time to answer each letter. Please write about bugs (AARGH!, "The typesetters blew it!"); extensions to the subroutine modules; and other modules.
Please write to:

Howard Franklin
c/o Golden Delicious Games
John Wiley & Sons
605 Third Avenue
New York, NY 10016

APPENDIX C

Typing Assistance

If you are going to type all our programs into your APPLE by hand, the following comments may help you read and enter the listings:

1. The modules should be saved on your disk just once, as they are, with no other program parts. That way you can always merge just the module with your program. You have to type the module only once!

2. We carefully used high-line numbers for the modules so they would not interfere with your programs. Programs should not go beyond line 10000, though they can be resumed at line 50000.

3. Avoid using variable names starting with W, X, Y, and Z in your programs, as they are used in the various modules.

4. If you have doubts as to what you are reading in the listings, here are some clues:

   The letter I is not used as a variable name. We did not even use AI or ZI. It's too easily confused with the number 1.

   The letter O is never used as a variable name, to avoid confusion with number 0. AO does not exist either.

   You may find variables names like A1 or B0 or C9.

5. The line numbers and blank REM lines provide a natural divider between program sections and thoughts.

6. If you are running out of memory space, you can delete all

or most of the REMs in the programs, but it's best that you leave them if you can, for future reference and changes. Delete on-line REMs first, then introductory REMs. On-line REMs annotate how the BASIC code works, while introductory REMs explain how to access the subroutines and make changes to the program.

7. If you are running out of memory space, you can delete parts of the INPUT MODULE and parts of the IMAGE MODULE that are not used. For example, since the game STARS uses only the letters S, T, A, and R, all other images in the IMAGE MODULE can be deleted.

APPENDIX D

Evaluating Programs

The phrase "user-friendly software" is being used often these days. As the quantity of available computer programs increases, people are becoming more selective about what they buy. They are looking not only for programs that will run on their computers, but also for programs that are easy to use. They are no longer patient with programs whose text scrolls off the screen, whose response requirements are awkward, or whose questions are ambiguous.

Throughout this book, we have made suggestions for programming conventions that are user-friendly. The INPUT routines, with their error traps and helpful error messages, are examples of user-friendly programming. The escape convention for exiting programs is another user-friendly routine.

This Appendix summarizes the suggestions already made and adds others. Use the following checklist to measure both your own programs and commercial programs for their user-friendly qualities.

DESIRABLE QUALITIES IN EDUCATIONAL SOFTWARE

Introduction/instructions at the same level as the activity.
Branching to avoid instructions.
Branching for "expert" mode.
Difficulty of task matched to required reading level.

Exit/interrupt information clearly stated.

Well-formatted, uncrowded screens.

Obvious choices of what to enter.

Consistent input pattern (use either INPUT or GET).

User-controlled flexibility in number of tries permitted.

User-controlled timing in instruction presentation.

User-controlled flexibility in difficulty of task.

Response for right answer more exciting than for wrong.

Helpful and non-negative responses.

Easily accessible "help" screens.

Error traps with helpful messages.

Frequent screen clears.

Consistent use of help and exit conventions.

Avoid These

Word wraparound.

Reading/responding at bottom of the screen.

Very "busy" screens.

Inadequate spacing.

Text scrolling off the screen (especially instructions).

Excessive flashing text.

Excessive use of sound, especially repetitive tunes.

Consider These

Is this a good computer application or could it be done better another way?

Does the thinking required to play the game match the learning experience being promoted? (Is two-step logic required in an otherwise simple game?)

Is it totally easy to operate the program? Learning to get around in the program is not usually the point of the game.

Index

Index